JAZZ *Life & Times*

This is a series of books about jazz artists, all of whom have made either a significant contribution or have had an impact on the jazz scene. Unlike some jazz books that concentrate upon the detail of the performers' lives or music, this series is concerned with much more. Here can be seen the social background into which the subject was born and raised and the environment in which his or her music was formed. The social, domestic, racial and commercial pressures that shaped the person are examined alongside an assessment of other musicians who may have influenced the artist or been influenced by them. Of course, the music is not overlooked and each book carries a discographical essay in which the artist's recorded output is summarized and analyzed. Well-illustrated, the Life & Times series of books is an important and long overdue addition to jazz literature.

Billie Holiday

HER
LIFE & TIMES

JOHN WHITE

Omnibus Press
LONDON/SYDNEY/COLOGNE

In the same illustrated series:
Louis Armstrong by Mike Pinfold
Gene Krupa by Bruce Crowther
Bud Powell by Alan Groves

First published in Britain in 1987 by
SPELLMOUNT LTD,
Tunbridge Wells, Kent, England

This edition published in 1988 by
OMNIBUS PRESS,
a division of Book Sales Ltd.

Exclusive distributors:
Book Sales Limited
8/9 Frith Street, London W1V 5TZ, UK.
Music Sales Pty. Limited
120 Rothschild Avenue,
Rosebery, NSW 2018, Australia.

To the Music Trade only:
Music Sales Limited
8/9 Frith Street, London, W1V 5TZ, UK.

ISBN 0-7119-1292-0
Order No. OP 44460

Series editor: Bruce Crowther
Picture researcher: Max Jones
Designed by: Words & Images,
Speldhurst, Tunbridge Wells, Kent
Printed & bound in Great Britain by
Anchor Press Ltd, Tiptree, Essex

CONTENTS

Acknowledgements   6

Introduction   9

Chapter 1   *FROM BALTIMORE TO HARLEM*   14

Chapter 2   *SIGNIFICANT OTHERS AND
             'STRANGE FRUIT'*   31

Chapter 3   *RACE PRIDE AND RACIAL
             PREJUDICE*   57

Chapter 4   *'DECLINE' AND FALL*   85

Chapter 5   *BODY AND SOUL*   109

Chapter 6   *FINE AND MELLOW*
             Lady Day on record   129

Bibliography   136

Index   142

ACKNOWLEDGEMENTS

I would like to thank the following friends for their help and support:
Bruce Crowther, Mike Pinfold, Michael Shera, Richard Palmer, Mike Bowen, Richard Gibson, Mike Somerton and Brian Ward.

The illustrations in this book come from the Max Jones Collection, the Frank Driggs Collection, Beryl Bryden, G. Schilp, Andre Sass, and from stills used to publicize films made or distributed by the following companies: Majestic, Paramount, BBC Television & TCB Releasing Ltd; and records made or distributed by the following companies: CBS, Columbia, Jasmine, Verve. Pictures are reproduced by courtesy of Ole Brask, *Ebony* Magazine, *Jazz Journal International,* the Maryland Historical Society, the New York Historical Society, the National Film Archive, Roy Burchell and *Melody Maker.*

Although efforts have been made to trace the present copyright holders of photographs, the publishers apologize in advance for any unintentional omission or neglect and will be pleased to insert the appropriate acknowledgement to companies or individuals in any subsequent edition of this book.

We are grateful for kind permission to quote lyrics as below:

Strange Fruit
Composer: Lewis Allan
c1959 Planetary-Nom (London) Limited,
222a Ladbroke Grove, London, W10 5FD.

My Man
Composer and author: Charles/Yvain/Pollack/Willemetz
c1920 Editions Salabert, France.
Ascherberg, Hopwood & Crew Ltd.

Without Your Love
Composer: R. J. Lange
Zomba Music Publishers Ltd.

FOR ASTRID

'Mom and Pop were just a couple of kids when they got married. He was eighteen, she was sixteen, and I was three.'
Billie Holiday

'To tell you the truth I was a little afraid of her. We were almost the same age, but Billie thought I was a square. And she could never understand why I didn't make a pass at her. But I was a very straight young man in those days.'
John Hammond

'She was the first non-white singer to sing with Artie Shaw's band, and also with Paul Whiteman. He was supposedly King of Jazz at the time. But to have one of the great black stars singing with your band wasn't acceptable. It was acceptable to go to Harlem and see black groups. It wasn't acceptable to go to a smart hotel and see black players.'
Bobby Tucker

'When Billie Holiday got busted in the forties, when she went to jail, it was headlines in the papers. You didn't hear so much when Anita O'Day got busted, or how many times. There were no rehabilitation places for black people, only prison.'
Betty Carter

'Billie Holiday used to sing in her day of "My Man Who Treats Me Mean" and that kind of material. But I don't see Negro men that way. I prefer to sing "Strong Man". I am a black woman and a married woman, and I no longer see trite songs as an expression of our social existence.'
Abbey Lincoln

'Sometimes you are afraid to listen to this lady.'
Imamu Amiri Baraka *(LeRoi Jones)*

INTRODUCTION

'Lady Day sang with the soul of Negroes from centuries of sorrow and oppression. What a shame that proud, fine, black woman never lived where the true greatness of the black race was appreciated.'

Malcolm X

'Lady Day has suffered so much in her life she carries it all for you.'

Colin MacInnes

Billie Holiday is widely acknowledged as one of the greatest artists in the history of jazz, a legend in her own lifetime and, nearly thirty years after her untimely death, a persisting and profound influence on popular music. To the perceptive British critic and musician, Benny Green, 'the primary fact about the career of Billie Holiday is its purity . . . For a woman to sing for nearly thirty years without once bowing to the demands of the world of popular music surrounding her sounds nearly impossible when we remember that most of her material was borrowed from that very world.' Yet Billie Holiday's art and artistry transcended the ill-defined boundaries of jazz and pop. As Frank Sinatra informed readers of *Ebony* magazine in 1958: 'With few exceptions, every major pop singer in the US during her generation has been touched in some way by her genius. It is Billie Holiday whom I first heard in 52nd Street clubs in the early thirties who was and still remains the greatest single musical influence on me.' (In a 1970 album, 'Sinatra and Company', Sinatra included a tribute to Billie Holiday—*My Sweet Lady*).

A prolific recording artist, Billie Holiday—'Lady Day'—also reached a wider audience through night-club and concert performances, radio and TV appearances and, towards the end of her career, European tours. The publication in 1956 of her harrowing, bitter autobiography, *Lady Sings the Blues* (written

Lady Day

with William Dufty), brought Billie Holiday a great amount of additional publicity—most of it sensational and unsympathetic. Yet even earlier, her court appearances and convictions for drug offences had contributed to a growing popular awareness of this remarkable and troubled black woman.

Long before her death Billie Holiday had achieved notoriety as well as fame (and some small measure of fortune). To her friends and admirers, Lady Day's visible decline—physical and vocal—in the last ten years of her life was a cause for concern and, ultimately, grief. Ironically, although the motion picture *Lady Sings the Blues* (1972), directed by Sidney J. Furie and starring Diana Ross in the title role, presented a drastically simplified and often distorted image of her private and public life, it also aroused the (continuing) interest of a younger generation in her peerless recordings. These are now readily available, from the 'classic' sessions of the 1930s and 1940s to the often painful but always moving examples of her work in the 1950s. Indeed, almost every month sees reissues of seminal items in the Billie Holiday discography as well as legitimate and boot-leg issues of concerts, club dates, studio rehearsals and radio interviews. (For an evaluation of Billie Holiday's recordings, see the Discographical Essay).

Billie Holiday was born at a time (probably in 1915 but the date is uncertain) when American race relations were at a low ebb. Despite the pioneering efforts of such civil rights organizations as the National Association for the Advancement of Coloured People (NAACP) and the National Urban League (NUL) to ameliorate the economic and political condition of American Negroes, fifty years after the formal ending of slavery persistent white racism (and indifference) had reduced blacks to an inferior caste status throughout the United States. The Emancipation Proclamation of 1863 ultimately destroyed slavery but left racism unaffected. American involvement in World War I—initially as a supplier of arms and materials for the Allies—produced a marked (but temporary) improvement in the lives of those blacks who found employment in the 'war industries'. Billie's mother, Sadie Fagan, got a job in a Baltimore factory making Army overalls and uniforms but, with the general laying off of black women workers at the end of the war, decided that she could do better working as a maid in the North.

When mother and daughter were re-united in Harlem in 1927, they quickly faced the onset of the great Depression although as Billie wryly comments: 'A depression was nothing new to us, we'd always had it.' As a black woman, and as a jazz singer, Billie Holiday would confront the realities of racial prejudice and discrimination, as well as male (black and white) domination in both her personal and professional life. These experiences were recounted by Billie to her friend and collaborator, William Dufty, a journalist, in *Lady Sings the Blues.* Billie's autobiography is a document every bit as revealing as Malcolm X's life story as told to Alex Haley, Claude Brown's account of growing up in Harlem: *Manchild in the Promised Land,* entertainer and civil rights activist Dick Gregory's *Nigger,* or the more recent appearances of

Billie in London, 1959.

autobiographical statements by such noted black American women writers as Maya Angelou, Angela Davis and Alice Walker. Billie Holiday's account of her own life and times—despite its factual inaccuracies and occasional hyperbole—offers a largely neglected (or slighted) but extremely informative description of the impact of poverty, deprivation, family insecurity and white hostility on the life of a gifted and sensitive black woman and, by implication, on the lives of her contemporaries. Fortunately for Billie Holiday, at critical

11

junctures in her life a succession of influential and well-meaning individuals offered her financial and artistic support, advice and inspiration. Throughout, *Billie Holiday: Her Life & Times* will consider these 'significant others', as well as the reflections of critics and musicians in the continuing reassessment of an artist whose supreme achievement was to transmute banality into beauty, the trite into the profound.

Billie's life and craft were well-served with the appearance in 1975 of John Chilton's fine biography, *Billie's Blues*. As a factual and sympathetic account of Billie's life from 1933 to her death, Chilton's book is extremely valuable. In addition, he also devotes four brief chapters to a consideration of her recordings. Like most critics, Chilton sees a steady decline in the quality of Billie's voice over the course of her career—an opinion which this writer does not endorse. But in ignoring Billie Holiday's formative years in Baltimore, Maryland, and in failing to set her life and its problems in the wider contexts of American and Afro-American culture, Chilton suggested the point of departure for this interpretative and complementary study. Chilton traces Billie's career from its beginnings at Monette's Supper Club in Harlem during the Prohibition era to her funeral service at the Church of St Paul the Apostle in New York City on 21 July 1959. But her story properly begins in Baltimore, a city 'celebrated' in verse by a black poet and a black blues singer:

> *Once riding in Old Baltimore*
> *Heart-filled, head-filled with glee,*
> *I saw a Baltimorean*
> *Kept looking straight at me.*
> *Now I was eight and very small,*
> *And he was no whit bigger*
> *And so I smiled, but he poked out*
> *His tongue, and called me 'Nigger'.*
> *I saw the whole of Baltimore*
> *From May until December:*
> *Of all the things that happened there*
> *That's all I can remember.*
> (Countee Cullen: *Color*)

> * * *

> *I want to tell you about a street I know,*
> *In the city of Baltimore,*
> *And every night about half past eight,*
> *The broads that's strollin' just won't wait,*
> *You'll find 'em every night on Pennsylvania Avenue.*

Getting Some Fun Out of Life. Still from 'Long Night of Lady Day'.

Now if you want good lovin', and want it cheap,
Just drop around about the middle of the week,
When the broads is broke and can't pay rent,
Get good lovin' boys for fifteen cents,
You can get it every night on Pennsylvania
  Avenue.
(Bertha Idaho: *Down on Pennsylvania Avenue*)

CHAPTER 1

FROM BALTIMORE TO HARLEM

'Baltimore is famous for rats.'

Billie Holiday

By the beginning of the twentieth century Baltimore, a city of 450,000 residents and situated on the rim of the South, had a larger black population (67,000) than any other American city except Washington D.C. But economic and educational opportunities for Negroes were severely circumscribed. Most black women worked as domestics or washer-women, while Negro men generally worked as drivers, porters, waiters and labourers. Before 1896 the city had never employed a Negro in any capacity. In that year the new Republican mayor announced that blacks would be hired for municipal jobs, but reassured his white constituents that Negroes would never be placed in positions where they could come into contact with white workers. In effect, the new policy meant that Negroes were employed as messengers, janitors and sanitation workers. In this last capacity the city sorely needed their services. Baltimore was the largest unsewered city in the country. Recalling his childhood in Baltimore at the end of the nineteenth century, H. L. Mencken, the iconoclastic journalist, remembered that his house had a private 'sink' connected to a 'private sewer' down the alley. The sink in Mencken's yard 'was pumped out and fumigated every Spring by a gang of coloured men who arrived on a wagon that was called an O.E.A.—i.e. odourless excavating apparatus. They discharged this social-minded duty with great fervour and dispatch and achieved non-odourifousness, in the innocent Aframerican way, by burning buckets of rosin and tar. The whole neighbourhood choked on the black, greasy, pungent smoke for hours afterward. It was thought to be an effective preventive of cholera and tuberculosis.'

Negro housing in Baltimore at this time was ramshackle and inadequate. Near the harbour, blacks and foreign-born immigrants lived in tenement slums. The worst slum was 'Pigtown', off Columbia Avenue (now Washington Boulevard). A reporter for the Baltimore *News* visited the area in 1892 and found: 'Open drains, great lots filled with high weeds, ashes and garbage accumulated in the alley ways, cellars filled with filthy black water, houses that are total strangers to the scrubbing brush . . . villainous-looking negroes who loiter and sleep around the street corners and never work; vile and vicious women, with but a smock to cover their black nakedness, lounging in doorways or squatting upon the steps, hurling foul epithets at every passer-by; foul streets, foul people, in foul tenements filled with foul air; that's "Pigtown".'

In 1908, the Baltimore *Afro-American,* a black newspaper, reported that racial segregation was on the increase in the city.

Whites were allegedly complaining about Negro attendance at free concerts held at the Peabody Institute, and were demanding the segregation of high school teachers at lectures sponsored by the Baltimore school board. The city's public schools were already rigidly segregated, although white teachers were given jobs in black schools—a policy that angered local black leaders. In the early twentieth century the Baltimore school system was one of the worst in the United States. Billie Holiday never progressed beyond fifth grade in Baltimore's dilapidated and segregated schools. But, as she ruefully observed, even that was progress. 'Mom was only 13 years older than me and had never gone to school at all.'

Like other major American cities Baltimore contained two distinct societies, white and black—largely separate and certainly unequal. In 1911 the segregationist thrust achieved a notable victory when an ordinance was passed which prohibited the sale or occupancy of property in all-white or all-Negro city blocks to members of the other race. Yet, despite this stratification based on colour, the city at large did not present an attractive face. The streets were paved with cobblestones and were noisy and dangerous to pedestrians and riders. With some exaggeration Mencken insisted that: 'In retired by-streets grass grew between the cobblestones to almost incredible heights, and it was not uncommon for coloured rag-and-bone men to pasture their under-nourished horses on it. On the steep hill making eastward from the Washington

Billie Holiday's Baltimore, early 1900s.

16

Monument, in the very heart of Baltimore, some comedian once sowed wheat and it kept on coming up for years thereafter. Every Spring the Baltimore newpapers would report on the prospects of the crop, and visitors to the city were taken to see it.'

As a child, Billie Holiday (born Eleanora Fagan) lived on Durham Street in East Baltimore, with her great-grandmother, grandparents, her cousin Ida and her two small children 'crowded into that little house like fishes'. Billie's mother was often absent working as a maid in Philadelphia and New York. Her father, Clarence Holiday, had been gassed while serving with the American Army in Europe during World War I. He had wanted to be a trumpet player but switched to the guitar after the injury to his lungs and worked with the bands of William McKinney, Fletcher Henderson and Don Redman. Clarence disappeared when Billie was still a baby, but was to resurface when she moved to New York with her mother.

Many young black Americans in the 1920s—most notably, Alex Haley who traced his ancestry back to Africa in the widely acclaimed book and TV serial *Roots*—learned about their slave past from older members of the family. Billie, as a young child, eagerly imbibed this oral history as retailed by her great-grandmother—her grandfather's mother. Billie discovered that the old woman had been a slave on a Virginia plantation. Its owner, a handsome Irishman named Charles Fagan, was on intimate terms with at least one of his female slaves. In addition to his wife and legitimate heirs, Fagan had sixteen children by Billie's great-grandmother who would relate her feelings at being owned, body and soul, by a white man.

An awareness of her slavery heritage—including her mixed blood, a suspicion of whites, and an ambivalent attitude toward black-white relations during slavery—remained with Billie throughout her life. After moving to New York as a teenager, Billie reflected on her great-grandmother's enforced role as a white man's mistress and slave. They did at least live in the same world night and day, unlike Billie and her mother who found the world of Harlem one that was made by white people but which they never saw.

Billie Holiday also grew up as a Catholic. Her mother, Sadie, appears to have been a devout woman, and Billie told Mike Wallace in an interview given a week before her famous 1956 Carnegie Hall concert: 'All I had was my Mom and my preacher—he used to come every Sunday' for dinner (and take the choicest offerings). Yet, as recounted in her autobiography, not all of Billie's exposures to Catholicism were comforting ones. When she was ten, Billie who had earlier encountered the unwanted sexual attentions of her cousin Henry—was raped by a neighbour in a house on the infamous Pennsylvania Avenue. After this traumatic experience she was sent to a Catholic reformatory in Baltimore. For an infraction of the rules, Billie was forced by the Mother Superior to spend a night in a locked room with the body of a dead girl laid out in a coffin. Already terrified of dead people—her great-grandmother had died in her arms after a stroke and, despite her protests, Billie had later been forced to view the corpse of her cousin Ida—'I screamed and banged on the door, so I kept the whole joint from sleeping. I hammered on the door until my hands were bloody.'

Father Peter O'Brien, pastor at St Paul's Church in New York City, had these episodes in mind when he spoke of his fascination with Billie and of their shared religion on John Jeremy's remarkable documentary 'The Long Night of Lady Day' (BBC TV 'Arena' production, 1985). In particular, Father O'Brien reflected upon the 'strange connection between the very seductive world of nightlife and jazz, and the sort of life that a certain kind of Catholicism can propel you toward'. Billie, he suggested, was trapped between two polarities 'filled with a kind of joy of living and, on the other hand, tortured and disturbed'. Although O'Brien considered that Billie's early years in Baltimore might have induced her later self-destructiveness, he was at a loss to understand where the 'joy' in her life came from.

In fact, a precocious love of jazz—specifically the records of Bessie Smith and Louis Armstrong—provided much if not most of the 'joy' in Billie's young life. By the age of six, she had begun working before school, 'minding babies, running errands, and scrubbing those damn white steps all over Baltimore'. (Paid a nickel by white housewives for the job, an enterprising Billie purchased her own cleaning supplies and asked for fifteen cents.) Among the errands she ran were those for a certain Alice Dean, the proprietress of a local brothel. Rather than accept payment Billie asked the madam if she could listen to Louis Armstrong and Bessie Smith on the victrola in the front parlour. Most of all she 'remembered' hearing Armstrong's *West End Blues*—the first time she had heard anyone sing without using words. (Billie's memory here must have been playing her false: Armstrong's famous recording was made in June 1928, after she had moved to New York.) In later years whenever she was asked to name the inspirations for her own vocal style, Billie invariably cited the two giants of jazz in the 1920s: 'I always wanted Bessie's sound and Pops' feeling.' In *Hear Me Talkin' to Ya'*, the valuable compilation of taped interviews with jazz musicians edited by Nat Hentoff and Nat Shapiro, Billie remarked that her early love of jazz did not meet with approval on the home front: 'Of course, my mother considered that type of music sinful; she'd whip me in a minute if she caught me listening to it. Those days, we were supposed to listen to hymns or something like that.' On his first visit to Billie's apartment in Harlem, in 1938, Leonard Feather, who became her life-long friend, asked Billie to play her recording of *Billie's Blues*. Her mother, Sadie Fagan Holiday, interrupted the performance with a story of how Billie would 'annoy an aunt with whom they lived by singing those . . . blues about "my man this and my man that"'. Billie was told sternly that a child 'had no business singing about such things'. But Sadie recalled fondly the first song Billie ever sang was *My Mammy,* which she would sing all the time.

Billie's recollections of the red-light district in Baltimore have a ring of authenticity and find parallels in the early lives of two other famous black singers—Ethel Waters and Ella Fitzgerald. In her autobiography, Billie remembered that a brothel was perhaps the only place where blacks and whites could meet in a natural way and that they certainly could not do so in church. Establishments like Alice Dean's were the only places fancy enough to have a victrola where she could hear the best records.

Ethel Waters (1896-1977), the entertainer, cabaret star and actress, grew up in Chester, near Philadelphia. Also a Catholic, parts of her autobiography bear a striking similarity to Billie Holiday's experiences in nearby Baltimore. An illegitimate child, brought up by her grandmother, Ethel lived in the red-light district of Philadelphia, off Clifton Street, 'in the old Bloody Eighth Ward'. Of mixed blood—her maternal great-grandfather was 'a native of India', and her great-grandmother a fair-skinned former slave, Ethel Waters records: 'I came to know well the street whores, the ladies in their sporting houses, the pickpockets, shoplifters and other thieves who lived all around us.' Like Billie Holiday in Baltimore, Waters ran errands for prostitutes, for whom she retained respect and affection. Black and white prostitutes in Philadelphia 'worked together, lived and slept together', and in a racially mixed area, prejudice was conspicuously absent, since 'all of us, whites, blacks and yellows, were outcasts there together'.

Ella Fitzgerald, three years younger than Billie Holiday, grew up in Yonkers, New York, acted as a look-out for the local brothel and, to earn extra money, ran numbers in the illegal, gangster-operated lottery.

Billie Holiday's formative years in Baltimore were bitter-sweet. There she had the first of her life-long encounters with racial prejudice in every area of daily life. She also endured various forms of rejection and humiliation from her family and public authorities, and became street-wise and sexually experienced beyond her years. Most importantly, however, she heard and responded to her 'first good jazz' in a brothel. And, like thousands of other Negroes throughout America in the 1920s, she also heard of another black city within a city, a glittering Negro Mecca.

During the 1920s a slice of Upper Manhattan Island west of the Harlem River, from 130th to 145th Streets, contained the largest and most famous black urban concentration in America. In the late nineteenth century Harlem had been an exclusive, all-white suburb of broad, well-paved streets and brownstone apartments—the homes of judges, politicians, businessmen and upper-middle class New Yorkers in general. With the extension of Manhattan's three elevated railroad lines between 1878 and 1881, Harlem became better connected with other sections of New York City. The construction of new subway routes into the section fostered frenzied speculation in Harlem real estate, the erection of too many buildings, and the inflation of land and property values. Realtors took advantage of this situation and, despite the initial protests of white landlords and residents, blacks began to move into Harlem in large numbers. As early as 1900 more than half of New York's black population had been born outside the state: by 1910 there were over 91,000 Negroes in New York City, including a constant influx from the West Indies. In one respect, Harlem was New York's equivalent to the growing black urban ghettos across the United States. In another, it was unique. An Urban League report of 1914 affirmed that Harlem was 'a community in which Negroes as a whole are better housed than in any other part of the country'.

After World War I, Negro churches moved into Harlem from other areas of the city, as did black fraternal and civil rights organizations, newspapers and social service agencies. The Jamaican-born Marcus Garvey attracted an enormous black following with his Universal Negro Improvement Association, which stressed black self-help, race pride, and the redemption of Africa from the hands of the occupying European powers. Other cults, sects and store-front churches flourished in Harlem, along with medical quacks and mystics. In the decade after 1918 Harlem also became, in the words of James Weldon Johnson, novelist, song-writer and civil rights activist, 'the intellectual

An emerging slum: Harlem before 1920.

and artistic capital of the Negro world'. And, he added: 'It is almost as well-known to the white world, for it has been much talked and written about.' A gifted generation of black artists, scholars, creative writers and intellectuals—W. E. B. Du Bois, Langston Hughes, James Weldon Johnson, Claude McKay, Jean Toomer, Countee Cullen, Paul Robeson and others—established themselves in Harlem and (with the support of white patrons) produced the creative outpourings of the 'Harlem Renaissance'.

Parallel with (but separate from) this black cultural ferment, Harlem in the 1920s had become the hub and inspiration of a flourishing Negro entertainment industry. Bessie Smith, Florence Mills, Ethel Waters and Bert Williams assumed the status of popular folk heroines and heroes—but were largely ignored by the leaders of Harlem's cultural establishment. Nathan Huggins, a black historian, makes the point that in slighting black contributions to the theatre and a still-evolving jazz music: 'It is ironic that a generation that was searching for a "New Negro" and his distinctive cultural expression should have passed up the only really creative thing that was going on.' Yet to a generation of whites in search of the exotic and the risqué, Negro music and theatre provided spectacle and excitement.

Theatres operated by blacks, featuring black entertainers and playing before black audiences, sprouted in Harlem during the 1920s. The popularity of the Negro stage soon spread into other sections of New York City. In 1921 the all-black revue, *Shuffle Along,* with music by Eubie Blake and Noble Sissle, opened on Broadway to enthusiastic audiences. By the end of the decade, whites increasingly flocked into Harlem night clubs and dance halls to see and hear such major jazz figures as Duke Ellington, Chick Webb, Fletcher Henderson, Louis Armstrong and Fats Waller. But it was during the 1920s in particular that Harlem and the Negro were in vogue. Not all blacks, however, welcomed the presence of white tourists or the racial policies of club owners. Langston Hughes, one of the few Negro writers to appreciate the significance of jazz as a distinctive Afro-American art form, recalled that whites began to come into Harlem in droves. 'For several years they packed the expensive Cotton Club on Lenox Avenue.' But Hughes objected to the Cotton Club's firm Jim Crow policy which encouraged gangsters and rich whites but frowned on black patronage, making exceptions only for such celebrities as Bill 'Bojangles' Robinson. (W. C. Handy, the composer of *St Louis Blues,* was once refused admission to the Cotton Club, while his music was being played

A street in still-fashionable Harlem in the 1920s.

22

inside.) Harlem's black residents, Hughes affirmed, disapproved of the Cotton Club's exclusionist policy 'in the very heart of their dark community', and resented 'the growing influx of whites toward Harlem after sundown, flooding the little cabarets and bars where formerly only coloured people laughed and sang'. Most offensive was the fact that these unwelcome strangers 'were now given the best ringside tables to sit and stare at the Negro customers—like amusing animals in a zoo'.

Black performers were also expected to conform to white-held stereotypes of the Negro as a sensual, primitive and savage being. Marshall Stearns has described a typical Cotton Club extravaganza of the 1920s in which 'A light-skinned and magnificently muscled Negro burst through a papier-mâché jungle on to the dance floor, clad in an aviator's helmet, goggles

Beautiful Billie—an early publicity picture.

and shorts. He had obviously been "forced down" in "darkest Africa", and in the centre of the floor he came upon a "white" goddess, clad in long tresses, and being whipped by a circle of cringing "blacks". Producing a bull-whip from heaven knows where, the aviator rescued the blonde, and they did an erotic dance. In the background, Bubber Miley, Tricky Sam Nanton, and other members of the Ellington band, growled, wheezed, and snorted obscenely.'

The enactment of Prohibition, in Harold Esman's phrase, 'the greatest experiment in mass repression man has ever known', with the ratification of the Eighteenth Amendment to the Constitution of the United States and the passage of the Volstead Act of 1919, made Harlem speakeasies and 'blind pigs' spiritous establishments for the non-abstemious, as bootleggers and hoodlums supplied the intoxicating liquors. During the 1920s also, Harlem became a leading centre of gambling and prostitution in Manhattan. Negro alderman George W. Norris noted in 1922 that there was 'a larger amount and more open immorality in Harlem than this community has known in years'. Two years later a black journalist concluded: 'It is a house of assignation . . . this black city.'

But to many black Americans Harlem offered glamour, excitement, an improved standard of living and job opportunities. Musicians, waiters, cooks, coat-room girls, doormen, cab-drivers and others made up a sizeable work force, all dependent on the continued operation of Harlem night spots. And, as the popularity of musical and theatrical entertainment spread through the black community, the Negro press began to devote more attention to these amusements than to the more reserved activities of the black churches and social organizations. Whatever the harsher realities of life in an increasingly over-crowded and white-controlled Harlem, throughout the United States blacks thrilled at the prospect of actually setting foot in black Manhattan. As described by the Negro journalist, Roi Ottley, Harlem during the 1920s had a special ambience characterized by 'gaiety, good feeling and the sound of jazz'. Daily life seemed to be syncopated to 'the clink of glasses and the thump of drums', the music of Fletcher Henderson and the voice of Bessie Smith. It was heaven on earth: 'Urchins were happily tricking dance steps on the sidewalks. Laughter was easy, loud . . . money seemed to flow from everybody's pockets . . . Harlem had entered an era of noisy vitality.'

Describing the inspiration of his famous composition *Harlem Airshaft,* Duke Ellington explained how much went on

there. 'You get the full essence of Harlem in an airshaft. You hear fights, you smell dinner, you hear people making love. You hear intimate gossip floating down. You hear the radio. An airshaft is one great big loudspeaker . . . You hear people praying, fighting, snoring. Jitterbugs are jumping up and down . . . I tried to put all that in *Harlem Airshaft*.'

For Billie Holiday, already captivated by the sound of jazz, Harlem was her first intended port of call in the Summer of 1927 (which saw Lindbergh's solo flight to Paris) when she 'made it solo from Baltimore to New York', to join her mother who was working as a maid in Long Branch. In the event, a bewildered Billie, wandering around Pennsylvania Station, was spotted by a white social worker and taken to a home run by the Society for the Prevention of Cruelty to Children. Re-united

Billie in New York, flanked by tenor saxophonists Ben Webster and Johnny Russell.

with Sadie after two weeks, Billie persuaded her mother to board her out in Harlem.

Her mother inadvertently placed her in 'a fancy apartment house off 114th Street', in the 'care' of Florence Williams, identified by Billie as one of Harlem's leading madams. Billie promptly became a prostitute, but (by her own account) following her refusal to service an influential (and dangerous) black client, was arrested, charged and put into detention for four months in a filthy, rat-infested correctional establishment on Welfare Island in the East River. Towards the end of her sentence Billie worked as a cook for the warden and his family. (Always alert to instances of racial discrimination, Billie asserted that ordinary black women—maids and cleaners—would be arrested on the street on their way home from work. In court it was simply their word against that of a 'dirty grafting cop'. If they could pay, they got off.)

After her release and a further short spell as a prostitute—she refused to give her earnings to the pimp who had been waiting for girls returning from Welfare Island, sending them instead to her mother—Billie worked as a waitress in Jamaica, Long Island. She recounts that she also 'started to sing' at the local Elks Club to 'pick up a little change'. Unfortunately, no other details are available of this significant step in her life.

By the time Billie rejoined her ailing mother in a small apartment on 139th Street, the onset of the Depression and continuing black migration into Harlem (by 1930 its black population was about 200,000) had combined to transform the Negro Mecca into a Negro Slum of the first order. If horses were still grazing in the streets of Baltimore by this date, the chairman of a housing reform committee could announce in 1927: 'The State would not allow cows to live in some of these apartments used by coloured people in Harlem.'

Housing conditions had rapidly deteriorated as overcrowding, high rents and low salaries (or none at all) produced congested and insanitary conditions. Where large apartments of six or seven rooms had served the needs of earlier white residents with large families and high incomes, they did not meet the needs of the black community in the 1920s. Few new houses were built in Harlem during the decade, and black residents resorted to such stratagems as taking in lodgers—often employing the 'Repeating' or 'Hot Bed System' whereby individuals alternated in sharing the same bed—or holding 'rent parties', glamorous in legend but often sordid and violent in reality, in order to survive. But conditions steadily worsened. Between 1923 and 1927 the death rate in Harlem was 42 per cent greater than that of the entire city of New York, with high fatality rates of mothers in childbirth and high infant mortality. Family instability led to crime and juvenile delinquency, while venereal disease, tuberculosis, narcotics and rickets (evidence of malnutrition) plagued the section.

Returning to New York in 1925, after an absence overseas, Langston Hughes found that 'unlike the whites who came to Harlem to spend their money, only a few Harlemites seemed to live in even a modest degree of luxury'. Instead, they took the subway downtown every day and looked for work. Hughes learned quickly how dependent black Harlem was on white downtown. No longer was 'Harlem a world unto itself'. Its famous night clubs and theatres were owned by whites, as were most of the stores. The experiences of Hughes and other writers,

composers and artists (as recounted in *Harlem USA*) were galling. Even the books of Harlem writers needed a downtown publisher. 'Downtown: *white*. Uptown: *black*. White downtown pulling all the strings in Harlem . . . Negroes could not even play their own numbers with their *own* people . . . Black Harlem really was in white face, economically speaking . . . Before it was over . . . poems became placards: "Don't buy where you can't work!". "First to be fired, last to be hired!". "God Bless the Child That's Got His Own!"' (*God Bless the Child* was the title of a song composed by Billie Holiday in 1941, but it spoke very much to her condition and that of her fellow Harlemites in the 1920s and 30s.)

When musician, composer and painter William R. Dixon came to Harlem from Massachusetts in 1934, his experience was similar to that of Hughes six years earlier. '. . . it never really occurred to me until I went "downtown" to high school, that every person I'd seen in Harlem: the butcher, the policeman, the man who came to read the gas meter, and even the vendor of fruit and vegetables in the block, were all white.' To a little boy, it seemed as if white people owned practically everything in Harlem. But, Dixon remembered, 'they . . . didn't own the music' that he heard all around him.

With her mother suffering from an unspecified stomach disorder, unable to walk or to work, and too ill to attend Mass on Sunday, an unemployed and desperate Billie learned that Clarence Holiday was appearing downtown at the Roseland Ballroom with Fletcher Henderson's orchestra. On several visits she managed to extract some money from Clarence—terrified at being identified as her father in front of the young women who hung around the musicians. With the rent overdue, Billie decided on other measures. One day, cold and hungry, she walked a dozen blocks of Seventh Avenue looking in every club and speakeasy for work. Finally, she stopped at the Log Cabin, run by Jerry Preston, and asked him for a job. She told him she was a dancer but a few steps sufficed to dispel that claim. Then she told him that she could sing. 'He said sing. Over in the corner was an old guy playing the piano. He struck *Travelin'* and I sang. The customers stopped drinking. They turned around and watched.' The pianist, Dick Wilson, then swung into *Body and Soul* and the patrons began to cry. Billie Holiday had moved her first audience. She collected eighteen dollars in tips and left. On the way home, she bought a chicken and 'mother and I ate that night'.

The legendary Harlem pianist and raconteur, Willie 'The Lion' Smith, has verified Billie's famous account, and also provided some additional information on the 'Log Cabin' which was a one-room basement speakeasy at 168 West 133rd Street, with space for about seventy people. Officially called the Patagonia Club, it became known as Pod's and Jerry's, after the proprietors. They were Charles Hollingsworth, nicknamed 'Pod' from his habit of calling people 'Pod-ner' and Jeremiah Preston, who was known as 'West Indian Jerry'. 'The Lion' recalled that: 'I worked on an old upright piano with yellow-chipped keys. The entrance door was decorated to make it look like you were going into a log cabin . . . when Prohibition was repealed, it was called the Log Cabin. It was there that Lady Day got her try out as a dancer and by accident wound up as a singer for Jerry Preston.'

When Preston offered Billie a regular singing job at eighteen dollars a week, conditions at home—including her mother's health—began to improve. And Billie herself began to attract attention. Artie Shaw, the white clarinetist and band leader, later to be Billie's employer, recalled his own experiences in Harlem at this time for the 'Arena' TV production 'The Long Night of Lady Day'. He would go and sit in at Pod's and Jerry's and, on one memorable occasion: 'Some little gal just walked in there and somebody said "Hey, Billie, why don't you sing some blues," and she got up and sang some blues. And she really had a sense of time and a sense of phrasing that was . . . jazz in the best sense of the word.' (Willie 'The Lion' Smith informed Shaw: 'That's Billie Holiday . . . she drinks too much and gets fired from too many jobs, but she can sing.')

Despite the ongoing Depression, Billie Holiday had 'arrived' in black Harlem; she had yet to be 'discovered' and promoted by 'white downtown'.

CHAPTER 2

SIGNIFICANT OTHERS AND 'STRANGE FRUIT'

'There's no damn business like show business. You smile to keep from throwing up.'

Billie Holiday

During her engagement at Pod's and Jerry's, Billie Holiday began working at other Harlem clubs along 133rd Street. Like other girl singers who moved from table to table in the course of their performance, she was expected to collect tips by lifting her dress to pick up the dollar bills left by customers by using her labia. After some humiliating failures in performing this degrading trick, Billie refused to continue the practice, and her less fastidious colleagues began to call her derisively 'Duchess' and, more often, 'Lady'—a title later expanded by Lester Young ('The President') into 'Lady Day'. By now Billie had grown into a strikingly attractive young woman. Spike Hughes, the British writer and musician, remembered seeing her at Monette's club in the early 1930s: '. . . a tall, self-assured girl with a rich golden-brown skin . . . Billie was not the sort you could fail to notice in a crowd at any time; in the cramped low-ceilinged quarters of a Harlem speakeasy she not only registered, but, like a gypsy fiddler in a Budapest café, she came over to your table and sang to you personally. I found her quite irresistible.' Hughes was not the only visitor to Monette's to be captivated by the sight and sound of young Billie Holiday.

John Henry Hammond, Jr, born into a wealthy New York family (his mother was a Vanderbilt) in 1910, had been drawn to the world of jazz from his childhood. By the age of twelve he was an avid collector of jazz rolls and records. In his autobiography Hammond recalls that although he was fascinated by all forms of music: 'The simple honesty and convincing lyrics of the early blues singers, the rhythm and creative ingenuity of the jazz players, excited me most . . . It was not long before I discovered that most of them—certainly all those I liked best—were black.' As a child, Hammond would bribe the family chauffeur to drive him around Harlem, and used to stand outside the Lincoln Theatre on 135th Street listening to Fats Waller playing the organ in the daytime stage show. In 1931 Hammond dropped out of Yale University, studied briefly at the Juilliard School of Music, and purchased a theatre on 2nd Avenue at 4th Street where he staged Negro shows with the orchestras of Fletcher Henderson and Luis Russell. A tireless promoter of black music, Hammond was also an active member of the National Association for the Advancement of Coloured People. He bitterly resented the exclusionist policies of Harlem clubs and the fact that, during the 1920s and early 30s, Negroes were not allowed to try on clothing in the white-owned department stores along 125th Street.

Among female singers, Bessie Smith was Hammond's first great (and lasting) enthusiasm. He was to record her for the OKeh label in 1933, and in the 1960s, together with Chris Albertson, Bessie's biographer, supervised the reissue of the 160 sides she recorded for Columbia, in five double LP albums. During the 1930s Hammond, as critic, record producer and executive, concert promoter and talent scout, launched the recording careers of Benny Goodman (who became his brother-in-law in 1942), Count Basie, and the brilliant pianist, Teddy Wilson. In 1938-9 Hammond staged (and recorded) the celebrated 'Spirituals to Swing' concerts at Carnegie Hall, which featured such performers as Goodman, Basie, Sidney Bechet, James P. Johnson, and the boogie-woogie pianists Pete Johnson, Albert Ammons and Meade Lux Lewis. (His later discoveries include Bob Dylan, Aretha Franklin and Bruce Springsteen.) He was to play an equally decisive role in the recording career of Billie Holiday. Early in 1933 Hammond stopped off at Monette Moore's club on 133rd Street, a regular call on his Harlem rounds. He was expecting to hear Monette herself, an accomplished blues singer. Instead, a young girl was substituting because the proprietor had got a part in a show on Broadway. The girl, Billie, 'was not a blues singer, but she sang popular songs in a manner that made them completely her own. She had an uncanny ear, an excellent memory for lyrics, and she sang with an exquisite sense of phrasing . . . Further, she was absolutely beautiful, with a look and bearing that were, indeed, Lady-like.' Hammond decided that night that she was the finest jazz singer he had ever heard.

Of John Hammond, who was to be such an influence in her

Lester Young. In music and in friendship Billie was closer to the Prez than anyone else.

musical life, Billie remarks pithily that although he came from a family rich enough to give him anything his only interest was jazz, 'so his folks thought he was nuts for hanging round with Negroes'.

In most accounts, including his own, it was John Hammond who discovered Billie Holiday, and certainly he was the person who launched her early recording career. However, Jack

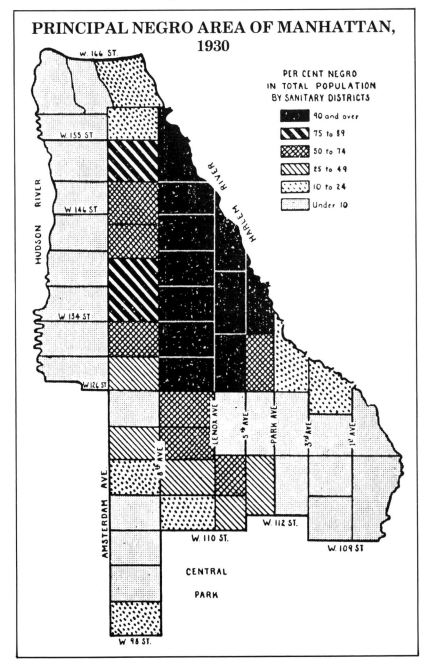

PRINCIPAL NEGRO AREA OF MANHATTAN, 1930

PER CENT NEGRO IN TOTAL POPULATION BY SANITARY DISTRICTS

90 and over
75 to 89
50 to 74
25 to 49
10 to 24
Under 10

Schiffman has suggested that it was one of the Apollo Theatre's stage hands, Bob Hall, an electrician, who 'found' Billie, and in his history of the theatre relates Hall's version of events. On his way home from work at night, Bob Hall would visit a little bar and nightclub, located near the Harlem Opera House and called the Alhambra Grill. After he became friendly with some of the musicians there, one of them asked Hall if he could get his 'old lady' a job singing. Hall approached the owner and asked him to let the girl sing. The musician's 'old lady' was Billie Holiday, who 'sang in the style that later became famous, and even though the club was small, she really tore it up'. The club's owner, Frank Bastone, kept asking Hall whether or not he should hire her and how much he should pay her. 'I think he ended up giving her thirty-five bucks a week,' Hall concluded, 'but that started her career.' Schiffman adds, 'It was only a short time later that John Hammond heard her, flipped over her voice, and set "Lady Day" on a road paved in equal measure with glory, loneliness, and heartbreak.' (Unfortunately, it is impossible to identify the musician who claimed the young Billie Holiday as his 'old lady'.)

Hammond went to hear Billie at various Harlem clubs—the Yeah Man, The Hotcha, the Alhambra Grill, Dickie Wells's, Pod's and Jerry's Log Cabin and other venues. In such surroundings he was further impressed by the fact that without amplification—most speakeasies were located on the ground floors of brownstone residential buildings and an inordinate amount of noise was not permitted—Billie could make a consummate virtue out of necessity. 'She would sing very quietly at various tables,' Hammond recalls, 'and sing the same tune differently at each table—just an unbelievable feat.'

For a time Hammond could only listen to and write about Billie in the musical press. He remembers that Billie was still unknown outside Harlem and, as a vocalist who did not play an instrument (unlike Louis Armstrong), was not regarded as a jazz performer. But, ever the enthusiast, Hammond made sure that his friends, like the actor Charles Laughton and his wife, Elsa Lanchester, as well as Benny Goodman (who had just begun to record for Columbia), heard Billie in person. Of this period Hammond relates: 'Billie's appeal to theatrical people, the gay crowd, and others outside the social norm was tremendous. Her message to them entirely escaped me, but it was strongly felt by others.' (On his frequent visits to Harlem Hammond had always steered clear of Bessie Smith's white patron, the socialite and erotic novelist Carl Van Vechten and his circle, because of their homosexual proclivities.)

With American Columbia wanting to make more records with Benny Goodman, and Goodman writing to feature Billie Holiday, Hammond was able to set up her first recording dates in November and December 1933, which produced *Your Mother's-Son-in-Law* and *Riffin' the Scotch*. In addition to Goodman, the studio band included the Teagarden brothers, Jack and Charlie, on trombone and trumpet, Gene Krupa on drums, and the Negro trumpet player Shirley Clay—the first time Goodman had recorded with a black instrumentalist. (For details of these and later recording sessions, see the Discographical Essay.) In her autobiography Billie recalled the occasion when Benny took her to the downtown studio. The sight of the microphone scared her. 'I'd never sung in one before, and I was afraid of it.' Fortunately she was encouraged by Ford Lee 'Buck' Washington of the famous Buck and Bubbles song-and-dance duo who was in the studio, who told her not to let the 'white folks' see that she was frightened, otherwise they would laugh at her. Neither of these sides—perhaps because of their banal lyrics and hokum arrangements—made any impact on the jazz market. Billie, who received only thirty-five dollars for the sessions, told Willis Conover, the Voice of America jazz broadcaster, in a 1956 radio interview, that on the atrocious *Your Mother's-Son-in-Law:* 'It sounds like I'm doing comedy. My voice sounded so high and funny.'

Not until nearly two years later did Hammond—now promoting the first recordings of the Benny Goodman trio in the United States and in England, as well as those of Billie Holiday—succeed in getting her into the recording studios again. Four titles were recorded on 2 July 1935: *Miss Brown to You, What a Little Moonlight Can Do, I Wished on the Moon,* and *Sunbonnet Blue.* They featured Teddy Wilson on piano, Roy Eldridge on trumpet, Ben Webster on tenor, Goodman on clarinet (apart from *Sunbonnet*), John Truehart on bass, and Cozy Cole on drums, and rank among Billie's finest records. Writing in 1977, John Hammond reflects on his astonishment at how casually they were able to assemble such stellar groups. 'It wasn't that we didn't know how great they were. We did. It was simply a Golden Age; America was overflowing with a dozen truly superlative performers on every instrument.' But business was poor, and all the musicians involved were happy to accept the union's scale payments.

Yet Hammond, as a writer for *down beat,* the first American musical publication to cover jazz and its Negro exponents, soon discovered in the late 1930s that although he was allowed to discuss the merits of blacks as performers, he was not permitted to write about them 'as a people who could not get a break because of their race'.

The year 1933 marked not only Billie Holiday's recording debut, but also the passage by Congress of the Twenty-First Amendment to the United States Constitution, repealing the Eighteenth, and only seven states—mostly Southern—voted to retain Prohibition. The astute John Hammond, eager to secure a permanent recording contract for Billie Holiday and other black jazz artists, realized the possibilities in this new situation of the, as yet, untapped juke-box market for promoting their music.

In 1934 Homer Capehart had brought out the first, somewhat cumbersome, juke-box; one year later, two hundred thousand were in existence, manufactured by several companies. With the ending of Prohibition, black bars across the United States

installed the new machines. Hammond realized that black bar owners were unable to find the right material to put in their juke-boxes, and was able to convince Harry Grey (head of the American Record Company) that 'It would be smart to make the pop tunes of the day acceptable to the black audience. They would be performed without arrangements, by the greatest soloists and a superb vocalist.'

As an added inducement, Hammond pointed out that four sides could be made for between $250-$300, with only six or seven musicians, and confided: 'The publishers are not going to crack down on us because you will have already covered their numbers with Eddy Duchin, Kay Kyser and the rest. They won't

Billie Holiday and Teddy Wilson: 'These sessions were pure joy.'

squawk if we take a little liberty with the tunes.' Grey accepted the idea and signed Teddy Wilson at $100 a week to produce the records, with Billie Holiday as the 'superb' vocalist.

The more than eighty songs which Billie recorded between 1935 and 1938 under Wilson's leadership (for the Brunswick and Vocalion labels) established her reputation. Hammond and

Wilson brought in the cream of available jazz instrument-alists—Ben Webster, Roy Eldridge, Buck Clayton, Johnny Hodges, Harry Carney and, most memorably, the tenor saxophonist Lester Young, to back Billie on these historic sessions. Although, as Hammond ruefully admits: 'The song pluggers went crazy when they heard the liberties we took with their songs and nobody really liked Billie Holiday,' her 30 June 1936 recording of *I Cried For You*—which also featured Jonah Jones, trumpet; Harry Carney, clarinet and baritone saxophone; Johnny Hodges, alto saxophone; Wilson, piano; Lawrence Lucie, guitar; John Kirby, bass; and Cozy Cole, drums—sold over 150,000 copies, five times as many as any of Wilson's previous records.

But Billie and Teddy were rarely given hit songs to record. In John Chilton's *Billie's Blues,* Teddy Wilson (in an interview with Don DeMichael) reflects on this aspect of Tin Pan Alley economics: 'In those days the publishers made the hits. They had what they called number one, number two and number three song plugs—the songs they were pushing. We never got into the plug tunes. We have our choice of the rest. That's why many of the songs we recorded you never heard anybody singing besides Billie.'

During the late 1930s Billie became friendly with Wilson's wife, Irene, and recorded three of her compositions—*I'm Pulling Through, Ghost of Yesterday* and *Some Other Spring.* If the Holiday/Wilson sessions did not capture the popular market, they captivated the musicians involved. Speaking to critic Nat Hentoff, Wilson recalled: 'These sessions were pure joy. I had never heard a girl with a sound like Billie's. She could just say "Hello" or "Good Morning" and it was a musical experience. And her singing, in a very integral way, was a reflection of her whole personality, her experience. What you heard when she sang was the very essence of her character ... she would often just sing her own melody, and it would come out better than what the song writer had come up with.'

Whitney Balliett, in the course of a 1982 profile on Teddy Wilson in the *New Yorker,* observed that part of the appeal of the Holiday/Wilson sessions is 'the contrast—not to say struggle—between his rhythmic rectitude and her alarming and irresistible rhythmic liberties. She sometimes sang entire vocals outside the beat while Wilson, in his accompanying solo, effortlessly gave her a reading of her exact location.'

Jo Jones, Count Basie's drummer, who was present on some of these recordings, had more culinary memories. 'Before the sessions Billie would go to the market, then put the pot on the stove with all those neck-bones and stuff, and we used to be in one hell of a hurry to finish the date, because we could smell that pot cooking all the way downtown.'

Although Hammond was delighted with the early Holiday/Wilson sessions, he sensed that they 'needed something extra to make their performances jell', and secured the services of trumpeter Buck Clayton and tenor saxophonist Lester Young, both from the Count Basie band, for the small group dates. (Basie himself, a consummate accompanist, was under contract to Decca, and therefore unavailable; in any case, Hammond had the services of the impeccable Wilson on piano.) Clayton, a lyrical and sensitive player and, according to Billie, 'one of the prettiest men I'd ever seen', provided one crucial ingredient; the other was supplied by Lester Young, who proved the perfect musical partner for Billie on such celebrated recordings as *This Year's Kisses, If Dreams Come True,* and *I'll Never Be the Same.* Young's dry, acerbic tone, cool and buoyant, was the antithesis of that of Coleman Hawkins, the founding father of jazz tenor saxophone playing. From their first recording date on 25 January 1937, which produced the aptly-titled *I Must Have That Man,* Lester's receptivity to Billie's pitch and phrasing produced some of the finest jazz ever captured on disc. Dave Gelly, in his study of Lester Young, writes: 'From the moment of that first meeting . . . an uncanny sympathy was forged between Billie and Lester. It was an instinctive musical understanding which went far deeper than a good working relationship; they didn't so much echo each other's thoughts as *think* each other's thoughts, and feel each other's feelings. There are many moments on these records when instrument and voice become one, exquisitely intertwined in a perfect balance of wit and passion.'

Lester and Billie were also complementary in other respects. During the 1930s both were regular smokers of marijuana, moving on to harder drugs (and hard liquor) later in their respective careers—and with equally dire consequences. In an article in *Jazz* magazine in 1959, John Hammond recalls that their first recording date 'was nearly cancelled when one of the American Recording Company officials walked in and sniffed the air suspiciously'.

Nicknamed 'Prez' (or 'Pres') by Billie, after Democratic president Franklin Delano Roosevelt, in Billie's words 'the greatest man around', Lester and Billie quickly became firm friends. Lester, terrified at the discovery of a rat in his New York hotel, sought safer accommodation. For a time he lived with Billie and her mother, and named her 'Duchess' and Billie

Lady Day and Prez.

'Lady'. In her autobiography Billie, who was to attend Lester's funeral a year before her own death, correctly forecast: 'Lester and I will probably be buried still wearing the names we hung on each other after he came to live with us.'

Although they saw less of each other in later years, Billie and Lester always had a special relationship. Several critics have seen a similar deterioration in their musical voices from the mid-1940s, as they both fought losing battles with drugs, alcohol and racial discrimination. But recently released recordings of Lester, performing in night clubs during the 1950s as well as several notable studio sessions when he was re-united with Teddy Wilson, indicate that Lester's 'decline', like Billie's, was only relative. Billie and Lester also appeared on concert and TV dates in the 1950s, most movingly on the CBS 'Sound of Jazz' TV broadcast in 1957.

Twenty-five years after their deaths, John Hammond, on 'The Long Night of Lady Day', reflected on the mutual attraction of Billie Holiday and Lester Young: 'They thought alike and they felt alike. I don't think there was any sexual relationship there—I think they just understood each other. It was so subtle and so close that I feel embarrassed even *talking* about it.'

41

In one of his rare interviews (with Chris Albertson in 1958), and printed in Stanley Dance's *The World of Count Basie,* the normally reticent and laconic Lester provided some succinct (but revealing) answers to Albertson's questions:

'When did you first meet Billie Holiday?'

'When I came to New York in 1934. I used to live at her house with her mother, 'cause I didn't know my way around. She taught me a lot of things, and got me little recording dates, playing behind her, and little solos, and things like that.'

'You're her favourite soloist.'

'She's mine too. So that's a draw.'

'I understand she gave you the name Prez, didn't she?'

'Yes, she did, and I gave her the name of Lady Day. So that was even.'

'I think she has said that her style of singing is formed after your style on tenor sax.'

'Well, I think you can hear that on some of the old records. Sometimes I listen to them myself, and it sounds like two of the same breed if you don't be careful, or the same line, or something like that.'

Max Kaminsky, the veteran white trumpeter, once visited Billie when she was staying in Boston. He presented her with an Orthophone record-player that had belonged to the guitarist Eddie Condon. Visibly pleased, Billie said: 'We'll dig some Prez.' As Kaminsky recounts, she listened to herself singing 'but when Lester's horn took off, Billie would take off with him . . . to hear her sing along with Lester Young, while he was playing a chorus, was something to make your toes curl. No words; she just scatted along with his tenor sax as though she were another horn.'

Certainly Billie always retained an affectionate high regard for the sessions of the 1930s made with Lester and other members of the Basie band—Buck Clayton, Harry Edison and Jo Jones. These sessions, often made at the end of a 500-mile bus trip, without music scores, and nothing to eat but sandwiches and coffee (or, in the case of Billie and Lester, a concoction of gin and port wine), were put together with almost insolent skill. Billie recalled that she would instruct Lester to play behind her for the first eight bars, then 'Harry Edison would come in or Buck Clayton and take the next eight bars', while Jo Jones was cautioned 'just brush and don't hit the cymbals too much'. In his autobiography, Buck Clayton writes of the sheer pleasure he experienced backing Billie's vocals: 'When she would record I would watch her mouth and when I saw that she was going to take a breath or something I knew it was time for me to play between her expressions . . . what we'd call "filling up the windows".' The contrast between these and later recording dates was pungently expressed by Billie: 'Now with all their damn preparation, complicated arrangements, you've got to kiss everybody's behind to get ten minutes to do eight sides in.'

Billie was exaggerating only slightly in her description of the apparent informality of the 1930s sessions. For BBC Radio 3, Teddy Wilson remembered more accurately that he would plan sketch arrangements, the length of a 78 record, set the tempo and assign each man a part so he would know what was to happen—when he was to solo, when Billie would sing, whether the accompanying improvisations should be in the background, or in the foreground. 'That's the sort of arranging I did for the groups, so each tune was fresh, and most of the songs—the musicians never saw them before we recorded them.'

Drummer Jo Jones has placed these sessions in another context. Before he and other Basie sidemen came to New York and began working with her, 'the only recording of Billie's that made any sense was *I Cried For You*. Prior to that they had no system, no format . . . ' With a wisdom born of long experience, Jones adds that the participating musicians were glad when the sessions were under Wilson's name 'because he was working with Benny Goodman, and so we'd have out checks all waiting for us, but if we were with Billie, we'd have to wait two weeks for the twenty dollars'.

In April 1934 Billie appeared at the Apollo Theatre in Harlem—where, a year earlier, Ella Fitzgerald had been 'discovered' and adopted by the black drummer Chick Webb, following her debut at the Harlem Opera House. The Apollo, at 125th Street near Eighth Avenue, had opened in 1914 as a burlesque house and in the early 1930s, under the management of Frank Schiffman, had begun to present vaudeville acts—singers, dancers, comedians and dance bands, offering new programmes every week. The Apollo's historian, Ted Fox, correctly observes that: 'To be a part of the Apollo audience was to be part of the show. This implicit link between the performers onstage created a charge like that between the two poles of a battery, and it electrified the atmosphere at the Apollo.' (The vibraphonist and drummer Lionel Hampton almost literally brought the house down one memorable night, when the balcony cracked under the strain of his cavorting fans.) An appearance at the Apollo could make or break a star, establish the reputation of a newcomer, or badly shake his or her confidence. Ralph Cooper, master-of-ceremonies at the Apollo, had heard Billie Holiday at the Hot-Cha Club and

excitedly informed Schiffman: 'You never heard such singing . . . it ain't the blues—I don't know what it is, but you got to hear her.' Schiffman agreed and Billie took another step forward in her career. Fifty years on, Doll Thomas, caretaker at the Apollo, told an interviewer for 'The Long Night of Lady Day': 'One of the most memorable recollections I have was when Billie Holiday made her first professional appearance on this stage . . . She knew she had to succeed, and everyone backstage—all the performers—were rooting for her, and the time came for her cue and she was overcome with fright.' Thomas then corroborated Billie's favourite story of having been pushed into the middle of the Apollo stage by the comedian Pig Meat Markham. After an unsuccessful attempt to hide her fears—'I couldn't control my knees'—Billie sang *If the Moon Turns Green* and, as an impromptu encore, *The Man I Love.* She remembered: 'The house broke up. There's nothing like an audience at the Apollo. They were wide awake early in the morning.' For the remainder of her life, Billie was an Apollo favourite.

Hazel Scott, the Trinidanian-born singer and pianist, then only fourteen years old, first saw Billie at the Apollo later in 1934. As Hazel recounted for Arthur Taylor's *Notes and Tones:* 'I was playing truant from school one Friday to catch the first show at the Apollo, because Schiffman would cancel most of the acts by the second show. All the Harlem school kids used to try and get there for the first show. Ralph Cooper announced: "Here's a lady with a . . . unique singing style—Miss Billie Holiday." I'll never forget. They used green lights on the stage and an amber light on her face. Her hair was tinted red . . . and she wore a white gardenia. She sang *If the Moon Turns Green,* and I flipped. I couldn't believe the way she sounded . . . I stayed through three shows just to hear her again.' That was not Hazel Scott's only exposure to Billie. Apart from hearing her on the juke box on her way home from school, Hazel was delighted when Billie began to visit the Scott house when she became friendly with Hazel's mother. Although closer to Hazel in age than to her mother, Hazel remembers: 'Billie was a woman already, and I was still a kid. She always protected me. She had a very fierce protectiveness where I was concerned.'

In 1935 Billie made a short appearance in the movie *Symphony in Black,* a brief feature for the Duke Ellington orchestra, directed by Fred Waller and filmed at Paramount's Long Island City studio. A young Billie (she was only 19) is seen standing under a window where her 'man' (the dancer Earl 'Snakehips' Tucker) is shown dancing with the 'other woman'

Harlem's Apollo Theatre where, as John Hammond remarked, 'Billie ruled the roost.'

(Bessie Dudley, his real-life partner). When Billie confronts her lover, he knocks her down and she sings a snatch of blues based on Ellington's *Saddest Tale*. A well-mounted and expertly edited film, Billie recalled it as a musical with only a minimal storyline but at least she was allowed to sing 'a real weird and pretty blues number. That was the good thing about the part. The rough part, of course, was that I had to play a chippie.'

She also remembered being badly bruised, rehearsing her dramatic fall to the sidewalk: 'I must have hit that hard painted pavement about fifty times before the man hollered "Cut."' All in all, Billie was less than enthused about her first film appearance, and saw only an extract from it one time at the studio. 'It was just a short subject, something they filled in with when they couldn't get Mickey Mouse. We'd have had to hire a private detective to find out where the hell it was playing.' (*Symphony in Black* was never a box-office draw although the sound track became available on Biograph Records in 1978.)

Under John Hammond's continuing guidance and with Joe Glaser, the impresario—and lifelong mentor of Louis Armstrong—as her agent, Billie worked in New York clubs and theatres from the mid-1930s. She appeared, briefly, in a revue

'I must have hit that hard painted pavement about fifty times . . . '—Billie.
Symphony in Black

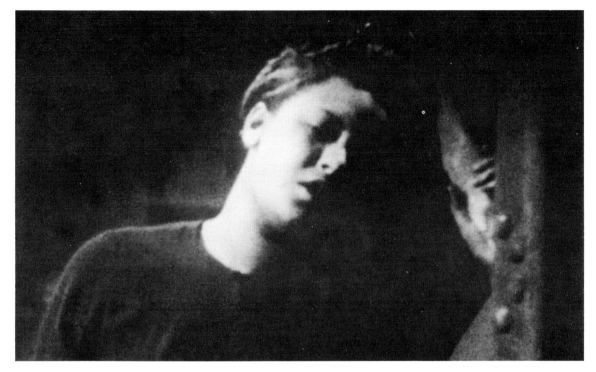

'Saddest Tale'.

at Connie's Inn, *Stars Over Broadway,* but was forced to leave because of ptomaine poisoning—to be replaced by her idol, Bessie Smith. Glaser booked Billie to work at the Grand Terrace Ballroom in Chicago in 1936, accompanied by the Fletcher Henderson orchestra. Ed Fox, manager of the Grand Terrace, unlike Schiffman at the Apollo, did not like Billie's style and told her so. A row ensued and Billie threw an inkwell at Fox's head. As she liked to recount with relish years after the event: 'Jesus Christ, they ran me out of Chicago. Ed Fox said "What the hèll, my Grand Terrace. Why the fuck should I pay you $250 (in fact, the amount was to have been $75) to stink up my god-damn show? Everybody says you sing too slow. Get out."' Glaser's advice was abrupt (he used to call his black artists *schwarzes*) and characteristic of his commercial approach: 'You've gotta speed up the tempo, you gotta sing hot stuff.' Billie's response was equally in character: 'I want to sing like I want to sing . . . that's my way of doing it.'

Later, when she was appearing at Cafe Society Downtown in New York, Fox came in with Glaser and, according to Billie, was so impressed by her enthusiastic reception that he pleaded with Glaser to let him book her for the Grand Terrace. Glaser told him that this was the same girl he had thrown out of the Grand Terrace and who had thrown the inkwell. 'He like to drop dead,' Billie recalled, but she asserted that she would not

47

appear at the Grand Terrace again, even if it meant she never sang anywhere. She vowed always to remember those who helped her on the way up but, equally, not to forget the others who were eager to push her down.

It was again the ubiquitous John Hammond who helped Billie 'on the way up' when, in 1939, he introduced her to another significant white figure who was to influence her career. Barney Josephson, a shoe salesman from Trenton, New Jersey, was an ardent jazz fan. Like Hammond, Josephson was a frequent visitor to Harlem on his business trips to New York and was appalled by the 'Whites Only' policy of the Cotton Club and other venues. In 1938 he decided to invest six thousand dollars of his savings in an interracial night club in Greenwich Village. Cafe Society Downtown, his first venture, was later paired with Cafe Society Uptown, at 128 East 58th Street. With space for 220 customers, admission charges of $2.00 for week-nights and $2.50 at weekends, beer at 65 cents a glass, and hard liquor at 75 cents, Cafe Society's slogan was 'The Wrong Place for the Right People'. Whitney Balliett writes of Josephson in *Ecstasy at the Onion:* 'His intent was simple and revolutionary, to present first-rate but generally unknown Negro and white talent to integrated audiences in honest and attractive surroundings. Lena Horne recently told *Essence* magazine: 'Josephson was a marvellous man, committed to hiring Black people and entertaining integrated audiences at a time when it wasn't considered normal . . . Cafe Society had the most wonderful audiences in the world—writers, scholars, entertainers.' It was at Cafe Society that she first met Paul Robeson and Walter White of the NAACP.

John Hammond encouraged Josephson's project and, with Benny Goodman and the booking agent Willard Alexander, put an additional $15,000 into the club after its first week of operations. Hammond also advised Josephson on promising performers for Cafe Society, including Hazel Scott and Lena Horne. Hammond was especially keen to bring Billie Holiday to Cafe Society where she would face a new audience in the company of first-class jazz musicians. In retrospect, Josephson believes that Billie 'really flowered' and 'sang her guts out' at his club. But relations between the two were not always harmonious. Josephson was white, and Billie was suspicious of all whites unless and until they proved their racial liberalism. Josephson's strictly enforced rule at Cafe Society was that there should be no use of drugs, but Billie was already on marijuana. Josephson had threatened to fire anyone who brought the drug near his club and, as he recalled for Kitty Grime, Billie would

Cafe Society, 1939: 'The Wrong Place for the Right People.'

be driven round Central Park in a hackney carriage between shows, indulging her habit. 'One night she came back and I could tell from her eyes that she was really high. She finished her first number and maybe she didn't like the way the audience reacted. Singers often wore just gowns and slippers, no underwear, because it's pretty warm under the lights. And Billie just turned her back, bent over, flipped up her gown and walked off the floor.'

Such incidents aside, Josephson generally sympathized with Billie and encouraged her to perform *Strange Fruit*, a surreal and savage indictment of lynching in the Southern states, by Lewis Allen, songwriter and composer. 'Lewis Allen' was the pen-name of Abel Meeropol (1903-86), who also wrote *The House I Live In,* a plea for racial and religious tolerance, sung by Frank Sinatra in a 1945 RKO movie short of the same title. (Meeropol and his wife adopted the sons of Julius and Ethel Rosenberg after they were executed in 1953 for allegedly passing atomic secrets to the Soviet Union.)

> *Southern trees bear a strange fruit,*
> *Blood on the leaves and blood at the root,*
> *Black bodies swaying in the Southern breeze,*
> *Strange fruit hanging from the poplar trees.*
> *Pastoral scene of the gallant South,*
> *The bulging eyes and the twisted mouth,*
> *Scent of magnolias, sweet and fresh,*
> *Then the sudden smell of burning flesh.*
> *Here is a fruit for the crows to pluck,*
> *For the rain to gather, for the wind to suck,*
> *For the sun to rot, for the trees to drop,*
> *Here is a strange and bitter fruit.*

Billie had reservations about performing the song: at first, she didn't grasp its irony, and then 'I was scared that people would hate it.' But Josephson, a staunch left-wing sympathizer, was determined that his radical/New Deal clientele should hear a 'protest' song delivered by a black singer. He insisted that she closed every show with it. The club lights were dimmed, with just one small pin-light on Billie, and all service was suspended. To Josephson, *Strange Fruit* was a piece of agitprop, to be staged dramatically. He explained to Kitty Grime his instructions after Billie's renditions—there were to be no encores and she had to walk off the stage. 'People had to remember *Strange Fruit*, get their insides burned with it.'

By the late 1940s right-wing newspaper columnists began to attack Josephson for his political views, and in 1950 he was forced out of the night club business. John Hammond writes: 'For a man who knew only how to sell shoes, Barney Josephson deserves lasting credit. He was a pioneer who remained true to his principles.'

For the remainder of her career *Strange Fruit* was firmly identified with Billie Holiday, and the song came to have more personal and profound meanings for her. In retrospect, she asserted that when Lewis Allen showed her the poem she immediately responded, seeing in its words those things that had killed her father.

Billie had been appearing at the Uptown House in New York

City when, on 1 March 1937, she received a call from a veterans' hospital in Dallas, Texas, informing her that Clarence Holiday was dead. As she later learned from the drummer Big Sid Catlett, Clarence had been touring the South with Don Redman's orchestra when he had contracted an unusual form of pneumonia. Because of Southern segregation and discrimination, Clarence, according to Billie's informant, had gone from hospital to hospital in an attempt to get help but none would take him in. As an American veteran, he was finally admitted to the Jim Crow ward of the army's facility in Dallas but died shortly afterwards. Rightly or wrongly, Billie believed

Cover Girl.

'it wasn't the pneumonia that killed him, it was Dallas, Texas'.

The story had a bizarre sequel. When Billie attended the funeral she discovered that in addition to his second wife, Fanny, Clarence also had a relationship with a white woman, who also attended the service with her two children—Billie's half brother and sister. Billie recounts that she was a lovely woman, very wealthy, and had met her father when he worked at Roseland. The children were being raised as white. Billie told her that she could do as she wished and 'if they could pass, let them'. Privately, however, she felt it was wrong not to tell the children the truth. Billie also drew her own moral from this unexpected encounter. The sight of her new-found siblings prompted the reflection that American customs were decidedly anachronistic. The Roseland management would have instantly fired any black who so much as looked at a white girl. But, as Billie wryly observes, the house rules 'worked in reverse . . . And here were the two kids to prove it.'

Billie's first recording of *Strange Fruit* was made in April 1939, for Milt Gabler's Commodore label, and the accompanying musicians included Frankie Newton, trumpet; Tab Smith, alto saxophone; and Sonny White, piano. John Hammond, who admits to never having liked the song itself or as a vehicle for Billie, felt that the executives at Columbia would think that the lyrics 'were too strong for its distributors to handle, particularly in the South'. Instead, he suggested that Billie should approach the owner of Commodore records.

Milt Gabler was also the proprietor of the famous Commodore Music shop, originally at 126 East 42nd Street, opposite the Chrysler Building and the Hotel Commodore; in 1938, he opened a second shop at 45 West 52nd Street. During the 1930s, Gabler's shop became a hangout for musicians, record collectors and jazz writers—John Hammond was a regular patron. In 1935, Gabler formed the United Hot Clubs of America, to promote the sales of jazz records including those on his own label. He also staged jam sessions at Jimmy Ryan's Bar on 52nd Street, and became an executive for Decca. Gabler heard Billie at the Band Box in New York, and became an immediate enthusiast. He signed her to a Decca contract and when Billie (revealing a weakness shared by many major artists) requested violins for some of her studio dates, Gabler promptly obliged—'I gave them to her. She was the first black girl to record with fiddles.' Billie's recording of *Strange Fruit* and her association with Gabler were turning points in her career. As Gabler told Kitty Grime, Billie did not become a recording star until her Commodore dates for him. Her recordings of *Fine and Mellow* and *Strange Fruit*

At the Ken Club, Boston, in 1944 with trumpeter Frankie Newton who appears on the original recording of Strange Fruit.

established her as a popular, rather than as a strictly jazz, artist with a limited audience. Ironically, her first 'hit' was *Fine and Mellow,* the reverse side of *Strange Fruit,* a blues, Gabler remembers, 'that we threw together on the back'.

Critical reaction to Billie's 1939 version of *Strange Fruit* was (and remains) mixed. Charles Edward Smith, the distinguished jazz writer and record reviewer, asserted in 1944 that Billie's 'sympathetic and faithful interpretation of the realistic lyrics . . . makes this one of the most effective of the "socially conscious" songs, its theme being lynching'. But writing in 1949, the jazz historian Rudi Blesh pronounced the record unsatisfactory on all counts: 'With its artificial jungle effects, and its unconvincing singing of artificial lyrics, it is a mood

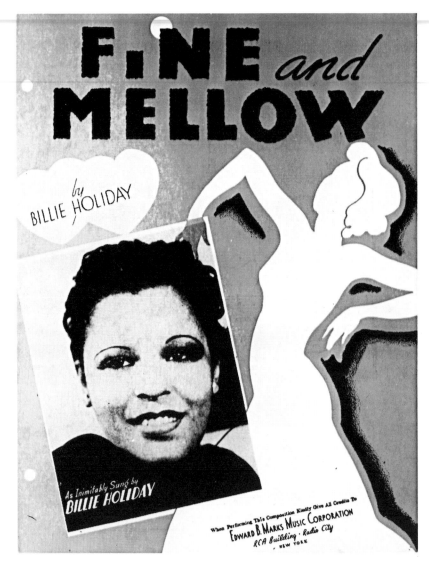

piece, an atmospheric bit of musical stuff too gauzy to hold a tragic content. The blues abound in social significance, but the real significance of *Strange Fruit* is that of the Negro adapting himself (*sic*) to our smart society while he sells out the birthright of his own great and original art.'

At this time Blesh was no admirer of Billie, whom he considered not a blues singer, rather 'merely a smart entertainer'. And he regarded her popular songs as 'trivial material at best, recorded with effete Negroes like the pianist, Teddy Wilson, or technically flashy but strictly non-jazz players, like white clarinetist Benny Goodman'. But, in a dramatic reversal of critical judgment Blesh, writing twenty-three years later, pronounced the Holiday/Wilson sessions masterpieces of small group jazz, and Billie an honours graduate of the 'blues school'. As for *Strange Fruit,* Blesh now considered it a 'grim song of death'; a nightmare song that Billie had made into her own so that no one else dared try it. 'She had been there. Lynching to Billie Holiday, meant *all* the cruelties, *all* the deaths, from the quick snap of the neck to the slow dying from *all* kinds of starvation.'

Blesh's second judgment of *Strange Fruit* was more astute than his first. Audiences rarely failed to respond to Billie's dramatic recitations of the song. Jack Schiffman, who had expressed strong misgivings about the performance of the song at the Apollo, recalls the effect of one such rendition before a black audience: 'If you heard it done elsewhere, you might have been touched and nothing more. But at the Apollo the song took on profound intimations. Not only did you see the "fruit" evoked in all its graphic horror, but you saw in Billie Holiday the wife or sister or mother of one of the victims beneath the tree, almost prostrate with sorrow and fury.' And as Billie finished her performance: 'A moment of oppressively heavy silence followed, and then a kind of rustling sound I had never heard before. It was the sound of almost two thousand people sighing.'

Throughout the 1930s and 1940s the NAACP pressed unsuccessfully for the enactment of a federal anti-lynching bill. Although the incidence of lynching declined in the Southern states by the eve of World War II, its sporadic occurrence— usually following unsubstantiated charges of Negro rape of white women—ensured that the images of *Strange Fruit,* as interpreted by Billie Holiday, would always arouse a response from black audiences.

In her autobiography Billie states that over the years she had many 'weird experiences' as a result of featuring *Strange Fruit.* 'It has a way of separating the straight people from the squares and cripples. One night in Los Angeles, a bitch stood up in the club where I was singing and said, "Billie, why don't you sing that sexy song you're so famous for? You know, the one about the naked bodies swinging in the trees."' Billie's response was immediate: 'Needless to say, I didn't.'

Lillian Smith, a Southern white opponent of racial discrimination, published her sensational novel *Strange Fruit* in 1944. An examination of segregation and white supremacy revolving around the clandestine love affair between a black man and a white woman, it quickly became a bestseller (and eventually sold over three million copies), was produced as a play on Broadway and, the ultimate accolade, was banned in Boston. Billie remembers that a few years after her Commodore recording of *Strange Fruit,* Lillian Smith 'told me that the song inspired her to write the novel and the play about lynching. You know what she called it.'

The most frightening description of Billie's emotional and personal involvement with the subject matter of *Strange Fruit* appears in the most recent volume of Maya Angelou's remarkable autobiography, *The Heart of a Woman.* The year before her death Billie, for a short time, became a frequent visitor to Angelou's home in California and became very attached to her young son, Guy. Just before she left for New York, Billie told Guy that she was going to sing *Strange Fruit* for him. Maya Angelou recounts: 'Billie talked and sang in a hoarse, dry tone the well-known protest song. Her rasping voice and phrasing literally enchanted me. I saw the black bodies hanging from the Southern trees. I saw the lynch victims' blood glide from the leaves down the trunks and on to the roots.' Guy did not understand the meaning of the phrase 'blood at the root' but Billie continued her recitation, and 'painted a picture of a lovely land, pastoral and bucolic, then added eyes bulged and mouths twisted, onto the Southern landscape'. Guy now wanted to know the meaning of 'a pastoral scene' and asked Billie to explain it to him. Billie's 'face became cruel and, when she spoke, her voice was scornful: "It means when the crackers are killing the niggers. It means when they take a little nigger like you and snatch off his nuts and shove them down his god-damn throat. That's what it means." The thrust of rage,' Angelou recalls, 'repelled Guy and stunned me. Billie continued, "That's what they do. That's a god-damn pastoral scene."'

Billie Holiday suffered, as Ralph Gleason has written, 'from an incurable disease—being born black in a white society . . .' Certainly by the 1950s, as a black woman and as a jazz singer Billie had already experienced—and resisted—the indignities of racial segregation and intimidation in the world of entertainment, and in the lives of black Americans at large. A closer examination of her encounters with racial and sexual prejudice in the 1940s and 1950s, when Billie emerged as a public performer, will help to explain her savage attachment to the brutalities exposed in *Strange Fruit.*

CHAPTER 3

RACE PRIDE AND RACIAL PREJUDICE

'America at large didn't know much about Billie Holiday . . . the only way that she could get into the front pages of the white newspapers was by getting into trouble, like getting arrested.'

Leonard Feather

'You can be up to your boobies in white satin, with gardenias in your hair and no sugar cane for miles, but you can still be working on a plantation.'

Billie Holiday

In embarking on a professional career as a jazz singer, Billie Holiday faced formidable odds on several related counts. From the 1920s, when it emerged as a new form of music and entertainment, jazz—while it quickly attracted the attention of the young—encountered the opposition of the American middle classes, black and white. Jazz was associated with sex, drinking, sensual dancing, poverty and vice. 'Moralists declared war on it immediately,' critic and historian 'Francis Newton' (Eric Hobsbawm) has observed, 'as usual with a splendid inability to make up their minds whether they objected to it because of its association with low life or the lower classes.'

Among Negro Americans of the 1920s and 1930s there were many who deplored jazz because of its 'debasement' of the black community, and deviation from the norms of Puritan rectitude and 'high' culture allegedly held by the white cultural establishment. As has been mentioned, this was very much the view taken by leaders of the Harlem Renaissance. Those Harlem intellectuals who did express an interest in jazz generally wanted to make it more 'sophisticated' and classically orientated. Above all, they wanted black creative artists to adhere to Western European forms and standards of cultural expression. They resented the equation between jazz, as performed by such early exponents as King Oliver, Louis Armstrong, Bessie Smith and Fats Waller, and Negro 'primitivism'. W.E.B. Du Bois, the outstanding black intellectual of the twentieth century, complained in 1940: 'Most whites want Negroes to amuse them; they demand caricature; they demand *jazz*.' As one of his biographers asserts, Du Bois's notion of a 'notable musical event was a black performer interpreting serious Western music, or a white composer or musician introducing African or Afro-American themes into his work'.

White educators and religious spokesmen took the lead in denouncing jazz, its practitioners and its tendencies, and were enthusiastically reported in the press. In 1922 the rector of the Episcopal Church of the Ascension in New York declared: 'Jazz is retrogression. It is going to the African jungle for our music.' Four years later the pastor of the Calvary Baptist Church in New York called jazz 'an agency of the devil', and proclaimed

With pianist Joe Bushkin at Decca Studios, 1946.

that 'jazz, with its appeal to the sensuous, should be stamped out'. An article in the *Ladies Home Journal* (November 1921) contained the intelligence that: 'If Beethoven should return to earth and witness the doings of a "Jazz" orchestra, he would thank heaven for his deafness . . . unspeakable jazz must go.' Writing in the *New York Times* in 1922, a physician explained: 'Jazz music causes drunkeness . . . sending a continuous whirl of impressionable stimulations to the brain, producing thoughts and imaginations which overpower the will.' In the same year the *New York American* carried a report that 'moral disaster' was overtaking hundreds of young American girls 'through the pathological, nerve-irritating, sex-exciting music of the jazz orchestras'. The Chicago Vigilance Association—the source of this information—had traced 'the fall of 1,000 girls in the last two years to jazz music'. In 1921 Mrs Marx Obendorfer, chairwoman of the Federation of Women's Clubs, published an article entitled 'Does Jazz Put the Sin into Syncopation?' She believed that it did and, as evidence reported that a survey of the lyrics of over 2,000 'best-selling songs' had judged only 40 'fit for boys and girls to sing together'. Jazz, Mrs Obendorfer pronounced, was in its original form 'used as the accompaniment of the voodoo dancer, stimulating the half-crazed barbarian to the vilest deeds'. Ridicule was also directed at the new music: in 1926, the *New York Times* carried the headline 'Jazz Frightens Bears' and, two years later, the sensational news that 'Cornetist to Queen Victoria Falls Dead on Hearing Coney Island Jazz Band'.

To hostile whites, the most damaging association of jazz was its identification with sexual immorality and the brothel. The white clarinetist Milton 'Mezz' Mezzrow recalled that in the 1920s, 'our music was called "nigger music" and "nice" people turned up their noses at it'. Billie Holiday both accepted and dismissed such charges, acknowledging that she was not alone in having heard her 'first good jazz in a whorehouse'. But Billie also argued that if she had heard 'Louis and Bessie at a Girl Scout jamboree', they would have made the same impression; had she heard them 'wailing through the window of some minister's front parlour', then she would have run free errands for the cleric rather than for Alice Dean.

Ironically, many jazz and blues players first heard a variant of instrumental and vocal jazz in the highly rhythmic, spontaneous and driving music performed in the black evangelical and fundamentalist churches in the 1920s and 1930s. T-Bone Walker, the blues singer, remembers that he first heard a boogie-woogie piano being played in the Holy Ghost

Church in Dallas, Texas. 'That boogie-woogie was a kind of blues, I guess. Then the preacher used to preach in a bluesy tone sometimes.'

The jazz bass player, Pops Foster, had a similar experience in various Southern churches: 'Their music was something. They'd clap their hands and bang a tambourine and sing. Sometimes they had a piano player, and he'd play a whole lot of jazz . . . They really played some great jazz on those hymns they played.'

Zora Neale Hurston, the noted black novelist, collected folklore materials for the New Deal agency, the Works Progress Administration (WPA) in Florida during the 1930s, and discovered that: 'In Jacksonville there is a jazz pianist who seldom has a free night; nearly as much of his business comes from playing for "Sanctified" church services as for parties. Standing outside of the church, it is difficult to determine just which kind of engagement he is filling at the moment.'

But black spokesmen—especially the clergy—echoed their white counterparts in condemning the anti-social and 'irreligious' connotations of jazz and secular entertainment in general. As early as 1883 the pastor of the Fleet Street African Methodist Episcopal Church in New York City asserted that dancing was 'of heathen origin' and had 'demoralizing effects on the Negro'. Adam Clayton Powell, Sr, pastor of Harlem's Abyssinian Baptist Church, warned in 1911 that 'the Negro race is dancing itself to death'. The editor of the prestigious *New York Age* noted in 1926 that Negroes wanted to maintain a 'high class of respectability' in their neighbourhoods, and attacked the indecency of Harlem rent parties which featured such celebrated exponents of 'stride' piano as James P. Johnson, Fats Waller and Willie 'The Lion' Smith. In 1939 the *Pittsburgh Courier,* another black newspaper, published letters from its readers complaining at the 'swinging' of Negro spirituals by jazz orchestras. One of its correspondents, the secretary of the Antioch Missionary Baptist Association in Natchez, Mississippi, wrote: 'Music as it is now sung, in gin shops, dance halls, on records, by orchestras, black and white, is truly a disgrace to the entire race.'

Lena Horne, a great admirer of Billie Holiday and an accomplished performer in her own right, remembers in her autobiography that she never really heard the blues but, rather, overheard them either on the radio from the next door apartment or, later, when she was appearing in clubs and theatres. 'The black middle class in Brooklyn and Pittsburgh did not think this kind of music was art. They thought it was

dirty, an unpleasant reminder of their low origins.' It was from the 'so-called white liberals' in the 1930s and 1940s that Lena Horne gained her appreciation of the blues as an Afro-American art form.

Similarly, the Negro novelist Ralph Ellison, author of *Invisible Man,* discovered that in the Oklahoma City of his youth, 'jazz was regarded by most Negroes of the town as a backward, low-class form of expression'. (Ellison was later forbidden to play jazz at the famous black vocational school, Tuskegee Institute in Alabama, under threat of expulsion.) In *Shadow and Act,* Ellison, a friend of the blues shouter Jimmy Rushing and the guitarist Charlie Christian, recounts that he grew up in a school where music was emphasized and classes given in the appreciation of 'the shorter classical forms'. Jazz, however, was considered beneath consideration by his teachers and the black clergy. 'Jazz and blues did not fit into the scheme of things as spelled out by the two main institutions, the church and the school.' But to Ellison and his fellow enthusiasts 'jazz and the public jazz dance was a third institution in our lives and a vital one'.

Billie Holiday, from a less privileged background than either Lena Horne or Ralph Ellison, recalls that, apart from the Baltimore brothels of her childhood, public dances were the only occasions when jazz music could be heard. She would go to as many dances as she could just to listen to the music.

If young women—black and white—were frowned upon for listening to jazz, they were certainly not encouraged to actually perform it. With the important exception of the piano, the instruments which parents believed it most fashionable for their daughters to learn—violins, flutes, cellos and harps—were those least employed in jazz combinations in the 1930s and 1940s. Yet, in fact, female jazz artists—instrumentalists as well as

vocalists—have made distinguished (if often literally unrecorded) contributions to the music from the 1920s to the present. They have, however, only belatedly received recognition (in the studies of Sally Placksin and Linda Dahl) and generally faced the indifference, if not the active hostility, of yet another male-dominated profession. As Linda Dahl writes: 'The assumption about women in jazz was that there weren't any, because jazz by definition was a male music.'

Whitney Balliett, a normally sympathetic and perceptive observer of the jazz scene, suggested in 1962, in a preface to an essay on the pianist/composer/arranger Mary Lou Williams, that there has been little in the jazz life to attract women. Long working hours and often primitive conditions on the road could hardly be said to appeal to feminine sensibilities. Moreover, Balliett argued, women themselves 'lack the physical equipment—to say nothing of the poise—for blowing trumpets and trombones, slapping bass fiddles, or beating drums'. Balliett's assessment may be correct in its first supposition, but slights the roles of women in jazz as instrumentalists, and ignores the extent of male prejudice as a factor in the equation. In February 1938 *down beat* magazine carried an unsigned article on 'Why Women Musicians Are Inferior', which contained the sneering assertion: 'Outside a few sepia females, the woman musician was never born capable of sending anyone further than the nearest exit.' It proceeded to argue that women, on the whole, were 'emotionally unstable' and therefore 'could never be consistent performers on musical instruments'. Such patronizing attitudes have not entirely disappeared. In conversation with Linda Dahl, Melba Liston, the gifted black trombonist/arranger/composer, recalled having been sent for by Dizzy Gillespie to join him on a State Department sponsored tour in 1955. Typical of the responses from the band was: 'Goddamn, Birks, you sent all the way to California for a *bitch*?' Gillespie asked Melba for the musical scores he had asked her to write and said: 'Pass it out to these muthafuckers and let me see what a bitch you are.' Gillespie's curt instruction to the band was: 'Play the music, and I don't want to hear no fuckups.' Liston relates: 'Of course they got about two measures and fell out and got all confused and stuff. And Dizzy said, "Now, who's the bitch! . . ." So after that I was everybody's sister, mama, auntie. I was sewin' buttons, cuttin' hair and all the rest . . . I was a woman again.'

Yet, as Melba Liston's comment indicates, even when female jazz musicians were accepted by their male colleagues, they were still expected to fill a maternal role. Helen Humes, who replaced Billie Holiday in the Count Basie band, commented to Stanley Dance: 'I would often pretend to be asleep on the Basie bus so the boys wouldn't think I was hearing their rough talk. I'd sew buttons on, cook for them too. I used to carry pots and a little hot plate around, and I'd fix up some food backstage or in the places where it was difficult to get anything to eat when we were down South.'

Sally Placksin points out that during the 1930s when all-women orchestras were in vogue, maintaining a 'feminine' image was so important that the brass and reed sections in one band 'applied Mercurochrome to their lips because lipstick would come off while they were playing'. Again, female vocalists with the large jazz and swing orchestras were often selected as much for their looks as for their musical talents. During the 1940s Anita O'Day (who possesses both good looks and one of the most distinctive voices in jazz) was not prepared to function simply as a sex-symbol. O'Day, who joined the Gene Krupa band in 1941 at the age of twenty-two, wanted to gain acceptance on the evidence of her musicianship alone and appeared onstage in tailored suits rather than revealing gowns, unwittingly giving rise to mistaken notions about her sexual orientation.

In one of the last interviews before her death in 1981, Mary Lou Williams offered another perspective on women in jazz. Responding to Stan Britt's question, she asserted: 'Yes, it should be OK for ladies to make it in jazz today. Mind you, they won't have had my opportunity. I was lucky . . . how many six-year-old girls do you know who've played jazz, sitting on the lap of someone like Willie 'The Lion' Smith? . . . how many women do you know who can go out on the road and not eat properly for 30 days? And how many women do you know will go back for sandwiches in a town where they're lynching blacks? I've been through hell at times.'

As her last comment indicates, black entertainers faced special dangers when they encountered the customs and practices of Southern racism. In her autobiography, Ethel Waters, who toured the South with Bessie Smith in the 1920s, recalled a visit to Atlanta, Georgia, (Mary Lou Williams's home town) when a strict curfew law ensured that all blacks were off the streets by midnight. The whites she encountered 'could tell I was from the North by my accent, and possibly my manner', and never lost an opportunity to remind her of her 'place'. What disturbed Ethel Waters even more than these incidents was the fact that Southern blacks, perhaps making a virtue of necessity, avoided confrontations with their oppressors. For her part, she considered the whites 'showering their scorn and contempt on other people because of their colour as odd and possibly feeble-minded, and the tip-off that they were scared to death of us . . . that three-quarters of the Southern Negroes should complacently accept all that contempt, upset me.'

Billie Holiday joined the Count Basie band in 1937, and the Artie Shaw orchestra a year later. In both organizations—the first black, the second white—she enjoyed the admiration and friendships of musicians but, like Mary Lou Williams and Ethel Waters, also experienced the prejudices and hostility reserved for blacks by the surrounding white society.

It was John Hammond who introduced Count Basie to Billie. As Basie told George Simon in 1971: 'Hammond took me by the arm up to Monroe's one night and said there was a little girl there he'd like me to hear.' In his autobiography, as recounted to Albert Murray, Basie remembered: 'I was really turned on by her. She knocked me out. I thought she was so pretty . . . And when she sang, it was an altogether different style. I hadn't heard anything like it . . . and I told John I sure would like to have her come and work with the band if it could be arranged . . . naturally John agreed because he already had the same idea . . . So he arranged it.' Following a short engagement in Montreal, Billie went on tour with Basie for eight months in 1938. Working conditions were far from ideal. As Billie remembered, the band did not possess proper uniforms, equipment or instruments and after travelling countless miles without sleep and with no time for rehearsals were expected to be great. There were other problems as well: Billie was accused of 'romancing' members of the band, which led to dissension. (In fact, Billie relates, she was 'scared of the cats in the band because they were messing with too many chicks on the road'.) Probably her only sexual relationship in the band was with the guitarist, Freddie Green.

Former members of the band have other memories of Billie's presence. Earle Warren, the alto saxophone player with Basie, in a conversation with Valerie Wilmer (reported in *Jazz Journal*) recalled that in 1938 when the band was playing college dates, the members would stay in private homes. 'We used to set up cooking quarters and have our meals collectively. Billie was always very helpful. She was a great cook and, like Lester, always jovial and entertaining, very seldom moody or obstinate.'

Trombonist Benny Morton also had fond recollections of Billie's tours with the Basie band which he related to John Chilton. 'If the guys played cards, Billie could play cards with them, if they shot craps, she could shoot crap . . . mind you, she used to win all the money . . . These people made their own fun because they needed it, a lot of the time these people were hurting inwardly, because the world was cruel to them . . . Billie laughed her life away, but I believe that this girl cried a whole lot too.'

Morton's assessment is correct. At the time, and in retrospect, Billie was acutely sensitive and alert to racial prejudice in all its guises. On one occasion the Basie band was staying in a small Southern town which did not even boast a 'coloured' hotel. Provided with accommodation and hospitality by a local black minister, Billie and her Basie colleagues discovered that one light-skinned member of the band was absent from the dinner table. Later, they saw him emerging from a white restaurant in the town but he pointedly failed to acknowledge them. Billie, enraged, confronted him in the street and yelled 'All right for you Peola!'—a scathing reference to the young black woman who tried to 'pass' for white in the 1934 movie adaptation of Fannie Hurst's novel *Imitation of Life*.

When Billie and the Basie band appeared in a Detroit stage show there were complaints from patrons about black musicians in close proximity to bare-legged white chorus girls. The presentation was quickly revamped and, as Billie caustically explains: '. . . when the chorus opened the show, they'd fitted them out with special black masks and mammy dresses. They did both their numbers in blackface and those damn mammy get-ups.' But Billie was forced to join Basie and his men in an additional humiliation when he was told that she was too 'yellow' to sing with his band and might be mistaken for white. 'So they got a special dark grease paint and told me to put it on.' Basie at first refused to comply, but reluctantly agreed in order to protect his band. As Billie remembered bitterly, 'I had to be darkened down so the show could go on in dynamic-assed Detroit.'

For contractual reasons—she was a Brunswick artist, while Basie was with Decca—Billie was unable to record with Basie. Three air-shots from performances at the Savoy Ballroom in June and November 1937, when she was appearing with the band (*Swing! Brother Swing!*, *I Can't Get Started* and *They Can't Take That Away From Me* on 'Billie Holiday: The Golden Years') indicate that she was the ideal female vocalist for this remarkable jazz aggregation. Basie himself told George Simon that Billie 'never worked any important location with us except the Savoy Ballroom. She was our first girl vocalist and she was beautiful to work with. I used to be as thrilled to hear her as

Count Basie. Billie's time with the Basie band was short, less than a year, but it was musically and educationally fulfilling.

the audience was'. On reflection, Billie preferred the Basie band's spontaneity and collective improvisation to the earlier, formalized arrangements she had heard Benny Goodman rehearse with his band. Basie had no need for expensive arrangements. 'The cats would come in, somebody would hum a tune. Then someone would play it over on the piano once or twice. Then someone would set up a riff . . . Then Daddy Basie would two-finger it a little. And then things would start to happen.' Billie's feelings in this regard were reciprocated by 'Daddy Basie': 'She fitted in so easily; it was like having another soloist. All she needed was the routine, then she would come in with her eyes closed—no cues or signals.'

Unfortunately, Billie's relations with the band's managers were less harmonious. Willard Alexander, the Basie agent, told *down beat* magazine shortly after she left: 'It was John Hammond who got Billie the job with Count Basie, and he was responsible for Basie keeping her. In fact, if it hadn't been for John Hammond, Billie would have been through six months sooner . . . The reason for her dismissal was strictly one of deportment, which was unsatisfactory, and a distinctly wrong attitude towards her work. Billie sang fine when she felt like it. We just couldn't count on her for consistent performance.'

For her part, Billie indicated to Hammond that she was tired of touring with the band throughout the South in buses without air-conditioning, being relegated to the few poor hotels that would take blacks and having to pay for her own gowns (and cleaning bills) out of the seventy-five dollars a week that she claimed she was receiving from Basie. In her autobiography, and with perhaps understandable exaggeration, Billie recounts that she had joined Basie's band to make some money and to see the world, but that for nearly two years she 'didn't see anything but the inside of a Blue Goose bus, and . . . never got to send home a quarter'.

In 1938 Billie appeared with Artie Shaw's orchestra in Boston—a signal event. Leonard Feather, who attended the performance, remembered that: 'For a black singer to be singing with a white band in those days was highly unusual.' Shaw, he felt, was taking a calculated risk in employing Billie, while for her: 'That was probably when some of the troubles began because she went through terrible humiliations, being discriminated against and segregated when she went on the road.'

Shaw, as mentioned, had first heard Billie at Pod's and Jerry's Log Cabin but, according to Max Kaminsky, hired her without an audition. A member of the Shaw orchestra at this time, Kaminsky relates that on the journey up to Boston he

had to reassure him that Billie would suit the band's style. When Shaw was late for the rehearsal, Kaminsky began to start the band on a new arrangement of *Yesterdays*. 'I asked Billie to sing the clarinet solo part to fill in for Artie, and she stood up in front of the mike listening sort of dreamily while we played the song through once. On the second time around she came gliding in, in the nick of time . . . While she was singing, Artie walked in, and he just stood there. He couldn't believe she was that good.'

Almost from the outset, and despite their strong mutual attraction, Billie's tenure with Artie Shaw was plagued by problems, tensions and, ultimately, acrimony. Informed by ballroom owners that Billie's style was not 'commercial' enough, Shaw told the band that she would have to leave unless they were prepared to help out with her salary. As Shaw trumpeter John Best recalled for John Chilton, the musicians were making about ten dollars a night and agreed to contribute ten dollars each week to keep Billie with the band.

Song pluggers also put pressure on Shaw not to allow Billie to sing their songs on the radio, because of her deviations from the written melodies. Also, Billie was not allowed to sit on the stand with the band or with its other singer, Helen Forrest. For these reasons Shaw began to feature Helen Forrest (who was white) more frequently and her relationship with Billie deteriorated rapidly. Yet Helen herself retained an affectionate regard for Billie. 'She was wonderful to me,' Helen told George Simon. 'She was always trying to help. I can remember what she used to tell Artie. "Why don't you let that child sing some more? And make her some more arrangements too!" She was a really great person.'

But such problems, real as they were, did not begin to measure up against the prejudice and discrimination which Billie encountered on her tours with the Shaw orchestra in the South. Soon, even the worst days with the Basie band 'began to look like a breeze'. Things reached a point where Billie, as she recounts, rarely 'ate, slept, or went to the bathroom without having a major NAACP-type production'. Although most of the band treated her well, she soon tired of repeated scenes in roadside restaurants where often she was not even allowed to eat in the kitchen. 'Sometimes it was a choice between me eating and the whole band starving. I got tired of having a federal case over breakfast, lunch and dinner.'

There was also the degradation of being refused access to toilets when the band bus made its only stop on a 600-mile journey. Finally, she said: 'To hell with it . . . I'd just

Artie Shaw, with whose band Billie endured the problems of touring.

ask the driver to stop and let me off at the side of the road. I'd rather go in the bushes than take a chance in the restaurants and towns.'

With heavy sarcasm, Billie reflects that in Detroit the Shaw orchestra played in the same theatre where she had been obliged to black up to work with Basie. On this occasion, the 'management never asked me to wear pink make-up to sing with a white band, but if they had, I wouldn't have been surprised'.

Billie's experiences as a female black singer with a white orchestra were unhappily similar to those of Lena Horne, who spent four months with the bandleader Charlie Barnet (a friend of Billie's) in 1941. As she relates in her own autobiography: 'Every time we'd walk down the street together . . . we'd run the gamut or cold eyes and hot tongues . . . it was just as humiliating for me when we passed other Negroes . . . I was acutely uncomfortable in restaurants.' When she learned that the band had a series of bookings in the South, Lena knew that she wouldn't be able to stand it. 'My nerves were completely gone. I couldn't sleep, I couldn't eat . . . when I'd glance down, I'd see that my hands were trembling.'

Black jazzmen also suffered as much as their female colleagues from the virulent racism that prevailed in America during a period when the federal government was notably inactive on the civil rights front. Frequently assaulted by members of the audience, black performers in the South rarely played in integrated surroundings. Edmond Hall, the clarinet player, recalls an engagement with the Claude Hopkins band in Birmingham, Alabama—until the advent of Dr Martin Luther King in the 1960s, the most segregated city in the Deep South. 'When we played there they had a rope right down the middle of the floor. There was white on one side and coloured on the other.'

Roy Eldridge, who joined Artie Shaw in October 1945, was refused admission to a dance engagement where his name was featured on the poster outside. Finally admitted, he played the first set trying to keep from crying. 'By the time I got through the set, tears were rolling down my cheeks. I don't know how I made it . . . Artie made the guy apologize that wouldn't let me in, and got him fired.' Embittered by such experiences, Eldridge concluded: 'When you're on the stage, you're great, but as soon as you come off, you're nothing.'

Artie Shaw was aware of Billie's volatile nature when confronted by racial bigotry, as well as the pervasiveness and subtle forms of Southern racial prejudice and etiquette. Recalling one such episode, he describes how he warned Billie to expect trouble in the South and promised to help her escape if things got out of hand. At one Southern location, Billie sang *Travelin'* with the band, to the obvious delight of the white audience who wanted an encore. One red-necked patron kept yelling 'Have the nigger wench sing another song', translated by Shaw to mean 'this sounds good, we like her'. Billie became very angry, leaned forward, and mouthed the word 'motherfucker' to the offending customer. Shaw recounts: 'Well, it looked like pandemonium. This guy saw her—he couldn't believe what he saw. He heard the word. And then she called him something else—some awful word came out of her, she was so mad. She used to get very salty with people like that.' (Shaw immediately put his preconceived plan into effect and Billie was whisked away in the band bus. 'Meanwhile, out on the floor, it looked like riot time.')

Billie experienced a Northern contribution to racial discrimination when she appeared with Shaw in the Blue Room of the (ironically-named) Lincoln Hotel in New York City in October 1938. As she informed a reporter from the Negro newspaper, the New York *Amsterdam News:* 'I was billed next to Artie himself, but was never allowed to visit the bar or the dining room, as did the other members of the band. Not only was I made to enter and leave the hotel through the kitchen but had to remain alone in a little dark room all evening until I was called on to do my numbers. And these numbers became fewer and fewer as the night went on.' Shaw's recollection is that the manager of the Lincoln complained to him that Billie was using the public elevator to get to her dressing room and that the hotel's Southern guests had objected. When he asked Billie if she would mind using the freight elevator: 'She looked at me. Her eyes glazed, you could see the old thing of the black person's persecution.' Billie asserts that the Lincoln episode was the final straw and that while she could understand such things happening in the South, she could not accept it in New York. She told Leonard Feather: 'What a hell of a thing to happen in a hotel named after Abraham Lincoln.' Like many other blacks, Billie felt that Southern whites were more open in expressing their racial animosity than were their Northern counterparts. 'A good cracker says, "I don't like Negroes, period" . . .' while hotels, radio networks and the like in New York exercised their discrimination surreptitiously.

As with her earlier rift with Count Basie's managers, Billie's well-publicized break with Artie Shaw after the Lincoln Hotel episode was the consequence of several factors: persistent discrimination, commercial pressures and Shaw's unavailing attempts as a white band leader playing for predominantly white audiences to secure equal treatment for his black vocalist. In an interview with Dave Dexter for *down beat* in November 1939 Billie gave her own version of the reasons why she left Basie and Shaw. 'I'll never sing with a dance band again . . . It

72

Advertising an appearance at New York's Paramount Theatre, 1941.

never works out for me. They wonder why I left Count Basie, and why I left Artie Shaw . . . I'll tell you why—and I've never told this before—Basie had too many managers—too many guys behind the scenes who told everybody what to do. The Count and I got along fine. And the boys in the band were wonderful. But it was this and that, all the time, and I got fed up with it. Artie Shaw was a lot worse. I had known him a long time, when he was sickly from hunger around New York, long before he got a band. At first we worked together okay, then his managers started belly-aching.'

There were also contractual problems (as with Basie). Billie was still under contract for Brunswick and made only one side with Shaw, the marvellous *Any Old Time,* recorded on 24 July 1938, issued on the Bluebird label and subsequently withdrawn. Billie claimed that Shaw failed to pay her for this date—a charge which he refuted.

Leonard Feather, writing for the British musical newspaper, the *Melody Maker,* in 1938, suggested that Billie's departure from the Shaw orchestra came about because: '(a) His new radio sponsors, the "Old Gold" cigarette people, refused to use her on the air—maybe because Billie smokes a different kind of cigarette and (b) she was made to enter the Lincoln Hotel, where the band plays, by the back door.'

Whatever the causes, Billie and Shaw patched up their differences in later years and he spoke warmly of her brief stint with the band. He told BBC producer Steve Allen in 1973 that 'my band was rather a strange place for her to be', because their music was unlike that she sang with others. Shaw believed that Billie became resigned to never being recognized by a wide audience and that her failure in this respect was a contributing factor in her later serious addiction to drugs. In 'The Long Night

Billie in concert with Art Tatum in 1944, with Duke Ellington's Barney Bigard in background.

of Lady Day' Shaw adds the reflection that from the moment she joined his band: 'The guys could hear the difference between the way she did a song and the way any other singer we'd had up to that time could. Naturally, they had a lot of respect for her musically; she had for us. People say, "Why did you hire her?" and I say, "She was the only singer around that could keep up with that band."'

During the early 1940s, in addition to her famous engagement at Cafe Society, Billie worked at other venues in New York City, including the Onyx Club, Kelly's Stable, the Downbeat Club (formerly the Famous Door), the Spotlight Club and other bars along 52nd Street, with various accompanists and backings. In the late 1930s and early 1940s, 52nd Street, between 5th and 6th Avenues, was New York's jazz strip. Traditional, swing, and the younger 'cool' and be-bop musicians performed in its assorted clubs and bars. Whitney Balliett, in *Such Sweet Thunder,* draws the following graphic picture of 'The Street' during its heyday, between 1940 and 1945. 'Its clubs ... frequently changed hands and locations. [They] occupied the ground floors of seedy brownstones and had interchangeable interiors. There was a small vestibule, with a coffin-sized coatroom, and, beyond, a bar along one wall. This area, which on Saturday nights resembled a football rally, gave onto a forest of postage-stamp tables, and at the end of the room, flanked by rest rooms and a nominal kitchen, was a tiny bandstand on which four men were comfortable and five a crowd. The decor ran to stamped-tin ceilings, tinted mirrors, maroon velour hangings, and water-stained plaster. The clubs were dark and smoky, the liquor was bad but cheap, and they smelled like abandoned caves. But they were the perfect places to hear jazz.'

For Arnold Shaw, its historian: "The Street" was 'the story of how Harlem came downtown—not only its music and dances, but its chicken and rib joints and its talented people. The Street embodies the struggle of black singers and musicians to gain their rightful place in white society.'

Billie Holiday, however, only remembered that most of the musicians who were 'swinging' along 52nd Street were white. Apart from Teddy Wilson and herself, who were appearing at the Famous Door, there were no black musicians in other clubs. Even if Billie's recollection was faulty overall there was some justification for her racial sensitivity, for as she succinctly observed: 'There was no cotton to be picked between Leon and Eddie's (33 West 52nd Steet) and the East River, but ... it was a plantation any way you looked at it.' Billie and Teddy were not allowed to mingle with the customers at the Famous Door and after their set was over they were obliged to go into the street or the alley out back.

It was during this period in New York that Billie began to listen to the legendary performer Mabel Mercer. The daughter of an American Negro and a white mother, Mercer was born in Staffordshire, England, and graduated from the vaudeville circuit to become a night-club entertainer. Mercer brought the art of dramatic yet subtle phrasing to a new height and, as Bruce Crowther and Mike Pinfold observe: 'Her influence is heard increasingly in Billie's performances as she adopted a more positive attitude towards the lyrics of her material. The casually-made masterpieces of the 1930s were overtaken by the dramatic performances of the 1940s.' Mercer herself told Whitney Balliett that in 1941, when she was appearing at Tony's on 52nd Street, 'Billie Holiday . . . came in so much that her boss got mad and told her she wasn't being paid to listen to me.'

The white pianist Johnny Guarnieri recalls playing an engagement at the Onyx Club on 52nd Street in 1943. An accomplished musician in his own right (and a descendant of the Guarnerius family of violin makers), he was astonished by Billie's consummate style. On their opening night Billie simply handed him some ragged lead sheets and said: 'Give me four bars.' Guarnieri remembers: 'I played four bars. But she didn't come in. Figuring she hadn't heard me or just missed her cue, I started over again. Suddenly, I felt a tap on the back of my head and I heard her say: "Don't worry 'bout me—I'll be there."' Billie, as he quickly discovered, liked to come in behind the beat, and did not need a pianist 'to make her look good'. Guarnieri, on reflection, believed that Billie had perfect judgment about tempi. In particular, she knew instinctively when to deliver certain songs in slow tempo. 'When you heard her do *I Cover the Waterfront*, you had to say that her draggy delivery was perfectly suited to the song.' To Guarnieri, Billie Holiday's greatest musical quality 'was not the one that everybody fixes on—the expression and the feeling—but her innately and absolutely perfect sense of timing'.

Singer Sylvia Sims remembered a more aggressive and non-musical side of Billie's 'timing' in early 1940s. Hanging out with Billie at the White Rose Bar in New York City during World War II, she watched two sailors deliberately burning holes in Billie's coat with their cigarettes. Once outside with the nautical offenders, Billie 'laid them flat'. When the police arrived she simply informed them sweetly: 'They attacked me.'

Club Downbeat, Chicago, 1939.

76

In her 1979 novel, *Sleepless Nights,* Elizabeth Hardwick describes Billie's artistically dramatic appearance during her 52nd Street years: '. . . the lascivious gardenias, worn like a large, white, beautiful ear, the heavy laugh, marvellous teeth, and the splendid head, archaic, as if washed up from the Aegean.' Hardwick also writes knowingly about other aspects of Billie's life and times. 'The sheer enormity of her vices. The outrageousness of them . . . Her ruthless talent and the opulent devastation. Onto the heaviest addiction to heroin, she piled up the rocks of her tomb with a prodigiousness of Scotch and brandy . . . Her work took on, gradually, a destructive cast, as it so often does with the greatly gifted who are doomed to repeat endlessly their own heights of inspiration.'

During the war years Billie also played short engagements in Chicago, St Louis and Los Angeles. It was at Billy Berg's Trouville Club in Hollywood, where she appeared in May 1942, that Billie met and became friendly with Orson Welles who had a keen interest in jazz. However, after they had been seen together a few times she received telephone calls telling her that her friendship was jeopardizing his career. She was also told that if the relationship persisted she would never appear in pictures. (Billie, who had chosen her first name after the film star Billie Dove, cherished a childhood ambition to be a movie star.)

It was also in Hollywood that Billie met Clark Gable who, true to his screen persona, stopped to help damsels in distress when Billie and a 'rich young blonde starlet' had a break-down when they were driving Billy Daniels's Cadillac. More significantly, while she was playing at the Trouville Club, Billie met the fledgling impresario, Norman Granz, who was to play a vital part in her career in the 1950s.

Billie also formed another friendship during the 1940s, and one which was to endure. As Lena Horne revealed to *Essence,* the black feminist magazine, in its May 1985 celebratory issue on 'Black Women', Billie could be both charming and considerate. When Barney Josephson, owner of Cafe Society, asked her to sing the blues, Lena replied: 'I don't know how to.' She continues: 'I loved the blues but I couldn't sing them. He said, "Now I want you to sing this song that Billie Holiday does." I refused. He insisted. That was Billie's song [probably *Fine and Mellow*] and I didn't want to associate myself with it.' Eventually, Lena went to Kelly's Stable, where Billie was working, and asked to speak to her. Billie appeared and 'I told her I'd heard people talk about her song *Strange Fruit* and how wonderful she was. I told her they wanted me to sing one of her songs, and I didn't want to because I could already see the divide-and-conquer thing that was happening.' Billie asked her if she had 'two babies'. Lena said she did. 'And you take care of them?' When Lena replied that she did, Billie said: 'Well . . . sing it. I don't care. Sing anything you want to open your mouth and try to do 'cause you've got to take care of your children. You have to live your life. I'll always be here if you want a friend.' Billie, who did not offer friendship (particularly to women) easily, was as good as her word. With modest understatement, Ms Horne continues: 'Here I was this not-very-talented chick, who only had great looks, singing at Cafe Society. Billie would defend me. She'd say, "Yes, she's learning to sing, and she's a good kid." If she saw me dating someone she thought was wrong, she'd tell me to leave the place. Hazel Scott and I . . . we'd go to hear Billie together, and that's one time we would settle down and not fight. Because here was this voice speaking for the people. Billie's friendship was a very lucky thing that happened to me.'

In their exploitation at the hands of Hollywood film producers during the 1940s, both Billie and Lena suffered severe affronts to their fierce pride as black women and black singers. Until the 1970s, the Hollywood image of blacks conformed to (and fostered) the widely held stereotype of Negroes as carefree, lazy, easily-frightened, comic, rhythmic and essentially child-like beings. Screenwriter Dalton Trumbo asserted that Hollywood unfailingly made 'tarts of the Negro's daughters, crap shooters of his sons, obsequious Uncle Toms of his fathers, superstitious and grotesque crones of his mothers, strutting peacocks of his successful men, psalm-singing mountebanks of his priests, and Barnum and Bailey sideshows of his religion'. (Although such portrayals have now become extinct in American films and television, largely as a consequence of the civil rights and Black Power movements of the 1960s, heightened black awareness and belated white sensitivities, they are still remorselessly projected in British entertainment—most abysmally in 'The Black and White Minstrel Show'.)

David O. Selznick's *Gone With the Wind* (1939), with its depiction of loyal and contented slaves (one character in the film talks about 'the simple-minded darkies') and their paternalistic white owners, offended the NAACP which was successful in having some of the more offensive scenes altered in the early phases of production. Ironically, the black actress Hattie McDaniel received an Oscar for her performance as Scarlett O'Hara's 'mammy' in the film. (In fact, most of McDaniel's roles from the 1930s to her death in 1952 placed her in similar servile situations.) But, as she told the young Lena Horne, Miss McDaniel, a dignified person in her off-screen life, felt forced to 'wear two hats' in order to work and look after her family: 'I put my handkerchief on and I'm the best mammy that they've ever seen, and when I come home I take that handkerchief off.' In Walt Disney's *Song of the South* (1946), the Negro actor James Baskette played the kindly Uncle Remus and was awarded a special Oscar in 1947 for his 'able and heart-warming characterization'. He was also the subject of an *Ebony* magazine editorial which attacked his 'Uncle Tom-Aunt Jemima caricature complete with all the standard equipment thereof: the toothy smile, battered hat, grey beard, and a profusion of "dis" and "dat" talk.'

Although Billie's idol, Louis Armstrong, appeared in several movies during the 1930s, more often than not he was forced to adhere to (and exaggerate) the stereotype of the black jazz musician as a cross between a savage and a clown—most glaringly in the 1943 MGM film version of the successful all-black Broadway show *Cabin in the Sky*. At one point in the film Armstrong appears in a leopard skin. Despite some glorious

musical sequences, *Cabin in the Sky,* as Daniel J. Leab asserts, perpetuated the images that had offended American blacks for decades. 'The movie contained the standard sequences of ecstatic psalm-shouting and jubilant crap-shooting. Black women were either old and dowdy or young and lascivious. The aides of Lucifer, Jr, spoke in ungrammatical dialect.'

Lena Horne, who appeared as 'Georgia Brown' in *Cabin in the Sky,* had already featured in an obscure all-black film, *The Duke is Tops* (1938), made especially for black audiences. Strikingly beautiful and light-skinned, Lena—under contract to MGM—was quickly subjected to the attentions of its make-up artists who darkened her skin to a shade called 'Light Egyptian' so that she could play opposite the Negro actor Eddie Anderson in a comedy melodrama. Lena Horne was an early and outspoken civil rights activist and believed, as she writes in her autobiography, that 'it was essential . . . to try to establish a different kind of image for Negro women' in films. But, as director Fritz Lang remembered, Louis B. Mayer, the head of MGM 'was at that time convinced that Negroes should be shown only as . . . menials of some description'. Reminiscing about her early Hollywood experiences during her sensational Broadway show in 1980, Lena Horne reflected that the 1940s film appearances, which included *Stormy Weather* (1943), had at least one positive outcome: 'All the black men in World War II wrote to MGM and said "Thank you for giving us our own pin-up girl. We can now put a picture in our foot-lockers," because a lot of places they were in . . . they couldn't put Betty Grable's picture in, but they were safe with my pictures.'

Ironically, when Lena hoped to get the title role in the Twentieth Century Fox production *Pinky* (1949), the story of a black girl light enough to 'pass' for white but who eventually renounces the deception, the part was given to Jeanne Crain, a white actress famous for her all-American girl characterizations. The dark-skinned Ethel Waters also appeared in the film as Aunt Dicey—yet another 'mammy' figure who is made to say that 'coloured folks had their place'.

With such precedents and practices it is hardly surprising that when Billie Holiday was offered a part in the film *New Orleans* (1947), produced by Jules Levey and directed by Arthur Lubin, it was as a distinctly subservient character. Billie thought that she would play herself and sing a few songs. But when she saw the script she discovered that the only available roles for black girls who made movies were either as a maid or a whore. Although she would sing in this movie, she would still be playing the part of a maid. As she observed: 'I'd fought my whole life to keep from being someone's damn maid.'

Filmed at the Hal Roach Studios in Hollywood, *New Orleans* also featured Louis Armstrong as a trumpet-playing butler, with a band that included Barney Bigard, clarinet; Red Callender, bass; and Zutty Singleton, drums; as well as Armstrong fronting a larger band and, in the finale, an appearance by the entire Woody Herman orchestra. Despite the presence of such prodigious jazz artists, the film's producers deleted or seriously edited large portions of the jazz soundtrack (now available in its entirety on *Giants of Jazz* GOJ 1025), the remainder being barely audible above the dialogue of an inane script. Originally the film was intended to depict the closing down of the notorious Storyville red-light district in New Orleans by the United States Navy, and the exodus of black jazz players to Chicago. In the finished version, as Dave Dixon writes in his sleeve notes to the *Giants of Jazz* LP: 'Instead of a film glorifying black music, the emphasis throughout . . . was on whether or not the young white opera singer portrayed by actress Dorothy Patrick would throw over her career and run off with the gambler restauranteer played by the handsome Arturo de Cordova.'

Advance publicity stills for the film promised 'The Low-Down of Old Basin Street . . . Cradle of the Music That Rocked the World'. And yet, as Red Callender recalled in 1984, the film's producers 'were actually frowned upon because they tried to integrate a film with blacks and whites on the same thing'.

Leonard Feather, reviewing the movie for *Metronome* magazine in 1947, noted caustically that it could not possibly give offence to the white South: 'Billie Holiday is (of course) a maid, Louis Armstrong talks to his horn, no Negro shakes hands with a white man, and the . . . racial overtones of the story are carefully muted . . . Until Hollywood stops pussyfooting on the race question, and makes a picture with the attitude that it doesn't give a damn whether the South shows it or not, there will not be any real movie about jazz.'

During the making of the film Feather had been invited by Armstrong to visit the set, and arrived in Culver City to discover Armstrong rehearsing his small band for one of the musical sequences. Feather wrote in *down beat* twenty years later: 'Louis had been instructed to familiarize himself with music parts that had been taken off recordings of *When the Saints Go Marching In; Maryland, My Maryland; Hot Time in the Old Town Tonight*, etc. Some of them had been transcribed from primitive New Orleans music by a research crew sent to Louisiana by the producer; others were regular records by Bunk Johnson. So the men listened to some of the records they were

82

supposed to "learn" from. As Armstrong, Bigard and the others were gathered around the machine, they erupted in roars of laughter at the welter of wrong notes, out-of-tune horns, and generally unspeakable non-music.'

Billie herself is scathing about the racism and hypocrisy both in and surrounding the picture. Ordered to visit the studio's drama coach, she learned 'twenty-three different kinds of ways' to say 'Yez, Miss Marylee. No, Miss Marylee'. The coach's job, Billie observed, was 'to brief me on how to get the right kind of Tom feeling into this thing'. According to Billie also, Dorothy Patrick 'wanted nothing to do with me', and accused Billie of scene-stealing. When Billie, frustrated and angry, began to cry, Louis Armstrong warned the crew: 'Better look out, I know Lady, and when she starts crying the next thing she's going to do is start fighting.' Understandably and sadly, on all counts *New Orleans* did not meet with Billie's approval, but she put a brave face on for Leonard Feather, telling him: 'I'll be playing a maid, but she's a really cute maid.' In her autobiography,

Louis Armstrong and pupil: New Orleans.

Billie remarks on the extensive footage of music shot for the film but which remained unused. She never made another movie. New-Orleans-born Danny Barker, guitarist, composer and author, adds: 'They made their pictures as authentic as they could get them, but they didn't put any of it in the movie . . . because they wanted the movie commercial. They showed the leading man posing for fifteen minutes, fixing his tie, while they should have been showing the people, the real thing.'

Billie's mother, Sadie, never saw her daughter 'star' in a Hollywood motion picture. In the Summer of 1945, when she was appearing at the Howard Hotel in Washington D.C. with her second husband, trumpeter Joe Guy, and their short-lived big band, Billie had a premonition (confirmed the next day) that her mother was dead. Their relationship, despite separations, heated disagreements and mutual recriminations, had been a close one. Billie returned to New York where Joe Glaser had made all the funeral arrangements. Because of her memories of her great-grandmother dying in her arms and her terror at the sight of dead bodies, Billie at first refused to view her mother's body. When she did so she was appalled to see that Sadie had been dressed in 'some king of angel-pink lacy shroud' instead of 'one of her good suits'.

Singer Carmen McRae, who acknowledges Billie as her inspiration and idol, also knew and respected her mother. McRae also attended Sadie Fagan Holiday's funeral and relates that on the return from the cemetery Billie told Joe Guy: '"Joe I don't have anybody in the world now except you." She needed somebody to say that to. She felt completely alone.'

By the time *New Orleans* was released, however, Billie Holiday faced even more personal and pressing problems than Hollywood's persistent parodies of black Americans, and the loss of the mother Lester Young had named 'Duchess'.

CHAPTER 4

'DECLINE' AND FALL

'You can get in just as much trouble by being dumb and innocent as you can by breaking the law. I've learned the hard way.'

Billie Holiday

'Vulnerable? Oh, like a child.'

Bobby Tucker

Drink and drugs (hard and soft) have been popularly associated with jazz musicians and the 'jazz life' from the 1920s to the present. Although drug users have always been a minority among jazz artists, the lives of such famous performers as Leon 'Bix' Beiderbecke (1903-31), Charlie Parker (1920-55), Lester Young (1909-59), Bud Powell (1924-66) and Art Pepper (1925-82) were prematurely curtailed because of their addiction to alcohol and/or drugs. Happily, other jazz notables—Stan Getz, Gerry Mulligan, Chet Baker, Anita O'Day—have successfully kicked their habits and regained, if not surpassed, their earlier creative powers.

Studies of professional jazz performers indicate that different drugs or stimulants have enjoyed a vogue at different periods. During the 1920s and 1930s, the preferred narcotic for 'vipers' appears to have been marijuana, known variously in jazz parlance as 'tea', 'reefers', 'gage' and 'muggles'. Coded references to marijuana appear in the titles of such recordings as *Viper's Drag, Reefer Man, Sendin' the Vipers, Muggles, Chant of the Weed, Golden Leaf Strut,* and *Tea and Trumpets.* Not surprisingly, many blacks deplored the use of marijuana as a threat to the race. In 1933 the black newspaper, the *Chicago Defender,* warned readers against the 'deadly puff' that left its users 'weak-minded and without will'. Again, the pioneering generation of New Orleans jazz players (with some notable exceptions) generally disliked dependency on alcohol or any form of drug. One veteran New Orleans player informed Jack

Buerkle and Danny Barker: 'We used to have a problem back in the '30s with musicians who didn't drink. They didn't smoke either. But, they smoked pot! That was a mystery to me. They got a big bang out of it. And, they could always find one another—these different pot smokers—seemed like they could tell one another. You couldn't tell 'em nothing! That's what they wanted, and they were supposed to be puttin' everybody on, and they were wiser than everybody else.'

Both Louis Armstrong (c1898-1971) and Bessie Smith (1895-1937)—Billie Holiday's acknowledged sources of inspiration—were unabashed marijuana smokers. In her 1933 recording of *Gimme a Pigfoot* ('and a bottle of beer'), Bessie substitutes a request for 'a reefer and a gang of gin' in the final chorus, and consumed large quantities of both substances during her turbulent life. Louis Armstrong's most authoritative biographer, James Lincoln Collier, asserts that he was only a moderate drinker and never used hard drugs. However, 'he came to use marijuana on a daily basis, until the end of his life'. John Hammond, returning from a trip to Europe with Armstrong in the 1930s, discovered that he heartily endorsed pot and purgatives as positive aids to healthy living. 'In those days Louis swore by two cures for all that ailed him. One was marijuana, the other Abilene water . . . a violent purgative. He believed that by keeping his system clean he would remain in good health.' Curiously, Louis considered alcohol evil and marijuana virtuous, and to Hammond's horror he smoked it constantly. Armstrong's marijuana habit never led him to try anything stronger, but in Hammond's opinion 'it did hurt him, for it enabled him to become the exhibitionist he became to the detriment of his genius'. Louis insisted that pot made him feel good, it relaxed him and, as he asserted to Hammond: 'It makes you forget all the bad things that happen to a Negro. It makes you feel wanted, and when you're with another tea smoker it makes you feel a special kinship.'

In a letter written shortly before his death, and published in the Max Jones-John Chilton biography, Armstrong (who was arrested and convicted of marijuana possession in California in 1931) offered some additional—if not entirely accurate—reflections on marijuana, its benefits and penalties. (The use of marijuana in the United States did not become a federal offence until the 1937 Marijuana Tax Act.) 'Speaking of 1931—we did call ourselves vipers, which could have been anybody from all walks of life that smoked and respected gage. That was our cute little name for marijuana . . . We always looked at pot as a sort of medicine, a cheap drunk and with much better thoughts than one that's full of liquor. But with the penalties that came, I for one had to put it down though the respect for it (gage) will stay with me for ever . . . One reason why we appreciated pot (was) the warmth it always brought forth from the other person . . . we always figured that pot could cut liquor any time. And being physic minded . . . we would take a good laxative . . . and keep our stomachs cleaned out, because that good stuff we were smoking gave you an appetite . . . We always used to say, gage is more of a medicine that a dope . . . if we all get to be as old as Methusela our memories will always be of lots of beauty and warmth from gage.' (Armstrong once wrote to an unreceptive President Eisenhower, recommending the legalization of marijuana.) Louis never claimed that marijuana actually improved his magnificent trumpet playing; Milton 'Mezz' Mezzrow (1899-1972), a decidedly second-rate clarinetist and saxophonist, did. In *Really the Blues,* Mezzrow offers the following hyperbolic account of the effects of his first 'reefer' on his playing: 'The first thing I noticed was that I began to hear my saxophone as though it was inside my head . . . I found I was slurring much better and putting just the right feeling into my phrases— I was really coming on. All the notes came easing out of my horn like they'd already been made up . . . all I had to do was blow a little and send them on their way. The phrases seemed to have more continuity to them . . . I felt I could go on playing for years without running out of ideas and energy.' Mezzrow's exaggerated claims—both as to the creative powers of marijuana and his own musicianship—are easily dismissed. No less an authoritative addict than Charlie Parker asserted in *Hear Me Talkin' to Ya':* 'Any musician who says he is playing better either on tea, the needle, or when he is juiced, is a plain, straight liar. When I get too much to drink, I can't even finger well, let alone play decent ideas. And . . . when I was on the stuff, I may have *thought* I was playing better, but listening to some of the records now, I know I wasn't. Some of these smart kids who think you have to be completely knocked out to be a good hornman are just plain crazy.'

The reasons for the prevalence of narcotics in jazz (or in any other area) are complex and seemingly contradictory. Several explanations, none of them entirely satisfactory, have been offered. Gary Kramer, in an important essay in *The Jazz Word,* after making the valid point that 'drug *use* and drug addiction are not synonymous' suggests that the social backgrounds of jazz musicians themselves provide one possible clue. 'From the twenties on, a high percentage of jazz . . . musicians have been

Negroes. The typical jazz musician either grew up in or lived most of his (or her) life in the Negro slum quarters of New York, Chicago and Detroit ... Even those jazzmen originally from the South, typically came to these ... Northern cities at an early enough age to come under the same environmental influences ... Certain oppressive features of life in slum neighbourhoods weigh heavily on a significantly large number of individuals living there. When the pressures become unbearable, these individuals become vulnerable to drug use and/or the associated pathologies of street corner society, all of which stimulate and promote one another: prostitution, sexual irregularities, gambling, rackets, gang-warfare, anti-authority behaviour etc.'

Kramer's thesis—that racial discrimination and poverty indirectly lead to drug use, if not to drug addiction—is provocative but incomplete. It fails to account for those middle-class musicians (many of whom were white) who turned to narcotics. His other suggestion—that an individual seldom begins to take drugs on his or her own initiative, but usually at the urging of a friend or acquaintance—is more convincing and, as will be seen, appears to have been at least partly the case with Billie Holiday. Similarly, Kramer's finding that psychiatrists regard the 'repeated use of either marijuana or the addicting drugs as an index to a long-established pattern of anxiety and maladjustment' appears to fit the facts of Billie's personality and experience almost too neatly. Her addictions, after earlier uses of marijuana and opium, were to alcohol and heroin—the staple narcotic of such 'modernist' jazzmen as Charlie Parker, Bud Powell and Fats Navarro.

Charles Winick, a psychotherapist and leading researcher into the use of drugs by jazz musicians, has suggested that there has been a symbiotic relationship between particular drugs and stimulants, and particular forms of jazz. The first excess attributed to jazz players was a heavy dependence on alcohol. Winick, in Nat Hentoff's *The Jazz Life,* suggests that New Orleans (and later, Chicago) jazz 'was generally outgoing and aggressive', and that 'alcohol has the effect of facilitating aggressive tendencies'. (More pertinent, perhaps, is the fact that jazz has usually been played in places where alcohol was readily available—legally or otherwise.) Winick also asserts that as jazz moved from the South to the North 'and became more light and swinging, alcohol began to give way to marijuana'. After World War II, the 'development of a more detached and cool jazz was simultaneous with the great increase in musicians' use of heroin, a drug which usually helps make the user more cool and detached'. This theory, attractive at first glance, ignores the fact that so-called 'modern' jazzmen, like Parker and Navarro, played extremely agitated and 'hot' music.

Whatever the reasons for their addiction, jazz musicians have been easy prey to drug pushers. By the mid-1940s, the narcotics traffic in New York City was concentrated on 52nd Street where, as pianist Billy Taylor recounted to Nat Hentoff: 'It became easier for guys pushing . . . dope or whatever to find their easy marks.'

Leonard Feather has elaborated on Taylor's impressions, confirming that marijuana was an accepted part of 'The Street's way of life. But during World War II the situation changed dramatically and around 1945 there were increasing numbers

of musicians who were hooked on heroin. As Feather went on to suggest, the link between hard drug addiction and organized crime was an intimate one. When prices rose, marijuana and other non-addictive drugs could be dropped by users; the crime syndicates preferred addicts whose habit could be depended upon to provide steady—and rising—profits for suppliers.

In an essay on narcotics in jazz, in *The Encylopedia of Jazz*, Feather concludes that they originally took hold on performers because of their desire to escape (or to hide) from racial and societal pressures, also because of feelings of 'artistic oppression'. But he also notes, as these pressures began to abate, it was 'from the narcotics themselves' that jazz players desperately tried to escape, only to be regarded (and treated) as criminals under the law. In conversation with Nat Hentoff, Gerry Mulligan ruefully reflected that the problems of his own generation with drugs 'came in part' from the way they were introduced to them. With hindsight, Mulligan considered that 'some sort of orientated introduction . . . and a method of understanding what was taking place in our bodies, instead of our having to search for drugs furtively and illegally' would have helped. Instead, he and his companions became totally involved with their habits and 'were thrown in contact with people whom we'd usually go out of our way to avoid'.

Billie Holiday's traumatic, painful and ultimately tragic involvement with hard drugs, and her frequent arrests for their possession, constitute the most harrowing and pitiful chapters of her autobiography—and of her short life. A marijuana smoker from her teens, Billie claimed that she was introduced to opium by her first husband, Jimmy Monroe, whom she married in 1941. She took to 'lying down' with Jimmy—already an opium addict—when their marriage began to fail, but asserts that he was no more the cause of her turning to narcotics than was her mother. Eventually she settled for heroin and developed a fierce and expensive habit. Anita O'Day, in her autobiography, recalls her first meeting with Billie in Chicago sometime during the 1940s, where the clerk of a Southside hotel arranged for them to pool their resources in order to purchase drugs. 'I wasn't only in awe of her singing, I was in awe of her habit. She didn't cook up on a spoon. Man, she used a small tuna fish can and shot 10cc into her feet. Later . . . she ran out of veins all over her body. So she used those on each side of her vagina.'

Sylvia Sims, a close acquaintance of Billie's, does not remember ever actually having seen her take drugs: 'It was only when she started wearing the gloves that we realized something was wrong.' Ralph Watkins, the owner of Kelly's

Stable on 52nd Street, told Arnold Shaw that initially he never had any trouble with Billie. But after she graduated from pot to heroin, she was 'a changed girl'—always borrowing money for her 'very expensive habit'.

In 1947 Billie (now divorced from Jimmy Monroe and married to Joe Guy) at Joe Glaser's urging, entered a private Manhattan clinic for a three-week course of treatment in an attempt to cure her addiction. Within three weeks of her discharge and, as she believed, now under close surveillance by agents of the Federal Narcotics Bureau, Billie and her accompanist, Bobby Tucker, were arrested in Philadelphia for drug possession.

The circumstances surrounding Billie's arrest are unclear— she provides an elaborate but confused account of the episode in her autobiography—but the upshot was unambiguous: she was sentenced for a year-and-a-day at the Federal Reformatory for Women at Alderson, West Virginia. In the course of his remarks at her arraignment on 27 May 1947 at the United States District Court in Philadelphia, the district attorney informed the judge: 'Miss Holiday is a professional entertainer and among the higher rank as far as income is concerned . . . She has given these agents a full and complete statement and came in here last week with the booking agent (Glaser) and expressed a desire to be cured of this addiction. Very unfortunately she has had following her the worst types of parasites and leeches . . . We have learned that in the past three years she has earned almost a quarter of a million dollars, but last year it was $56,000 or $57,000, and she doesn't have any of that money. These fellows who have been travelling with her would go out and get these drugs and would pay five and ten dollars and they would charge her one hundred or two hundred dollars for the same amount of drugs. It is our opinion that the best thing that can be done for her would be to put her in a hospital where she will be properly treated and perhaps cured of this addiction.' (Bobby Tucker was not charged and he was quickly released. Billie, who had befriended Bobby's mother, said at the time: 'Bobby Tucker? The strongest thing he ever had in his life was a Camel cigarette.')

In passing sentence on Billie, the judge was only partly moved by the district attorney's special pleading on her behalf. She was, the judge asserted, appearing as 'a criminal defendant' and was 'not being sent to a hospital alone primarily for treatment'. Medical treatment would be available at Alderson, but she stood 'convicted as a wrongdoer'. In conclusion, the judge expressed the hope that 'within the time limit in which you are to serve, you will rehabilitate yourself and return to society as a useful individual and take your place in the particular calling which you have chosen and in which you have been successful'.

En route to the reformatory by train, in the custody of two fat white matrons, Billie began to suffer withdrawal symptoms—sickness and diarrhoea—and was given a shot of heroin to keep her going, the last she would have until her sentence was over. In 1947 Alderson was a strictly segregated institution (although the inmates worked together) and about half the prisoners were black. They lived in 'cottages' with 50-60 girls in each, and the races were totally separate at meal times, in the chapel and cinema. But, Billie discovered, there were liaisons between some of the girls that crossed the colour line. On the way back from the movies, prisoners did not have to march in Jim Crow formation and, as it was usually after dark, advantage was taken of this sole opportunity for lovers of different races to make fleeting contact—often little more than holding hands.

After a four-week quarantine period, Billie worked in the Alderson kitchens, washing dishes and peeling potatoes, and then became a 'maid' in the camp piggery 'for a herd of damn squealing pigs. I'd never seen a damn pig in my life before'. Later she looked after one of the 'cottages'—lighting fires, cleaning windows, polishing floors and preparing meals. As Billie described her functions, she became a sort of Cinderella. In retrospect she recalled that the worst part was the final locking of the door at night. Always, this would start her thinking of the time when she was locked in the institution with the body of a dead girl.

At Alderson Billie was given the standard IQ and aptitude tests. Her 'Admission Summary' recorded:

> Rates best in languages and vocabulary
> Poor factual knowledge
> Has done singing and housework
> Seems inconsistent in her reasoning
> Low average intelligence
> Assigned to cottage maintenance
> Attends religious services regularly

On the whole, Billie appears to have found life at Alderson tolerable, and certainly a considerable improvement over Welfare Island. Unable to obtain heroin or any other drugs, she confined herself to cigarettes and, on one occasion, attempted to make bootleg whiskey. Generally cooperative with the reformatory's staff, Billie came to respect the warden, Helen Hironimus, who did the job because 'She believed in what she was doing. After church ... she would always come by the hospital where the girls were kicking dope ... She'd bring flowers and give them to the girls having a rough time.' After her release from Alderson, Billie recalls that Mrs Hironimus attended one of her concerts in Philadelphia. 'She had left her job, couldn't take it any more ...' After a few weeks at Alderson, Billie (who also expressed her concern at 'getting fat') wrote to Leonard Feather, asking him to contact Joe Glaser on her behalf: '... he has my money and I wrote three letters asking for some. I can only spend ten dollars a month but I can use that green stuff even here.' Painfully aware of the forcible separation from her public, Billie also suggested that Feather call Glaser 'and see what he intends to do about some good publicity for me, I've had so much bad stuff written and I do think he should do something so that people don't forget me, after all a year is a long time for one's public to wait.'

In 'The Long Night of Lady Day', Virginia McGloughlin, secretary to the warden, remembered Billie's confinement and her behaviour. 'She really went into the woodwork here, and at some point made up her mind that she was going to do her time and get out as fast as she could ... It's almost impossible to say how quiet she was, considering the fact that she was a well-known person. But to my knowledge, she never sang a note.' Billie corroborates this last statement in her autobiography. And Billie rarely played her own records in Alderson, although the inmates did, taking advantage of the many copies of her recordings sent to her from friends and admirers outside. Jean Allen, Billie's 'correctional officer' at the institution, remembers that she was 'generous' and also 'quiet, lady-like [and] matter-of-fact'. By her own account, Billie made only one close friend among the inmates, a girl called Marietta from San Francisco, who taught her to knit.

Billie was released on parole from Alderson on 16 March 1948, having served nine-and-a-half months of her year-and-a-day sentence. After a short recuperation at the home of Bobby Tucker's mother in Morristown, New Jersey, Billie began to rehearse for her 'Welcome Home' midnight concert at Carnegie Hall. Accompanied by Bobby Tucker and a rhythm section, Billie sang twenty-one songs and gave six encores to the delight of a packed audience. And *down beat* magazine reported: 'Whether or not her voice is quite as perfect as a year ago didn't matter a whit to the 3,000 disciples.' What these 'disciples' were apparently unaware of was that Billie had inadvertently stuck a large hat-pin in her head just before the second set, lost a large amount of blood, steadily weakened throughout her performance, and promptly collapsed after her third curtain-call.

But Billie's difficulties were more serious than a temporary loss of blood. After her conviction for drug offences, she was unable to sing in New York clubs because of the 'cabaret card' rule under which the police were authorized to license performers and could ban anyone convicted of narcotics offences. Permits were granted by the police department and the Alcohol Beverage Control Board. Dating from the era of Prohibition, anyone with a police record was barred from holding a liquor licence. Billie's application for a cabaret card was refused. She could appear in theatres, perform before an audience of juveniles, work on radio or TV, and appear in venues like New York's Town Hall or Carnegie Hall. But she was banned from bars and any club with a liquor licence—the very places where she had been used to making her living.

For a time, she managed to survive, playing club dates outside New York, and working out the remainder of her recording contract with Decca. In July 1948, Billie appeared with the Count Basie orchestra and other artists for a six-week residency at the Strand Theatre in New York, as added attractions for the showing of the motion picture *Key Largo*. (Three months earlier, she had opened in a show at the Mansfield Theatre called 'Holiday on Broadway', with Bobby Tucker as her accompanist, other jazz musicians and supporting acts. Despite a favourable notice in the *New York Times,* the show closed after three weeks.)

As at earlier points in her career, Billie needed—and was to receive—the support of a white patron and businessman, who could keep her alive as both a performer and a recording artist. When she had been appearing at Billy Berg's in Hollywood, Billie, as has been mentioned, became friendly with a young white man who, she recalled, 'had a good mind and loved jazz'. The young man in question used to tell her: 'John Hammond thinks he's something . . . Someday I'm going to be really big, and when I do, I'm going to do something for Negro jazz musicians.'

Norman Granz, this incipient jazz entrepreneur, was born in Los Angeles, and attended UCLA, while working part-time as a quotation clerk at the Los Angeles Stock Exchange. After a medical discharge from the army in 1943, he worked as a labourer at the Warner Brothers Studio and then as an MGM film editor. Granz frequented the Hollywood night clubs featuring jazz performers and was angered that blacks were not admitted as patrons. As he later told Leonard Feather: 'I remember once when Billie Holiday was complaining that some of her friends had come to see her and they weren't allowed in. She was crying and everything: it was a real drag.'

Granz persuaded Billy Berg to allow him to stage a series of weekly jam sessions at Berg's club, at which there would be no dancing—since the music was all-important—and blacks would be admitted. From these inauspicious beginnings—the musicians received only six dollars each—Granz formed his touring troupe of jazz artists under the banner Jazz at the Philharmonic (JATP), named after the Los Angeles Philharmonic Auditorium where he staged his first major concerts in 1944. They featured, among other players, trombonist Jay Jay Johnson; tenor saxophonist Illinois Jacquet; guitarist Les Paul; and pianist Nat King Cole; and were also recorded for posterity by the enterprising producer. By the mid-1950s, JATP tours had covered the United States, Japan and Europe with such artists as Coleman Hawkins, Lester Young, Charlie Parker, Oscar Peterson, Stan Getz, Roy Eldridge, and Ella Fitzgerald—all of whom began to record exclusively for Granz's several record labels. In 1944 Granz and Gjon Mili produced the brilliant jazz short (10 minutes) *Jammin' the Blues,* which won an Academy Award nomination. It featured such musicians as Lester Young, Illinois Jacquet, Harry Edison, Red Callender and Jo Jones actually playing the music heard on the soundtrack, where earlier Hollywood productions had recorded music and pictures separately. In 1947 Granz organized a benefit concert for Billie Holiday (still in Alderson) at Carnegie Hall.

For jazz musicians, white and black, Granz was (and remains) a benevolent despot with the interests of his performers firmly at heart. Dizzy Gillespie, a long-serving member of Granz's stable (and today a recording artist for Granz's magnificent Pablo label), asserts in his biography: 'The importance of Jazz at the Philharmonic is that it was the original "first class" treatment for jazz musicians. Norman Granz gave jazz musicians "first class" treatment. You travelled "first class", stayed in "first class" hotels, and he demanded no segregation in seating. Norman insisted that tickets be sold without regard to race, first come, first served.' Granz himself asserts that his early concerts and tours were more reformist (if not radical) than musical in their purpose. '. . . the whole basis of forming Jazz at the Philharmonic was initially to fight discrimination. It wasn't formed just to do jazz concerts . . . the whole reason for JATP, basically, was to take it to places where I could break

Norman Granz. One of several white men (John Hammond, Milt Gabler, Barney Josephson were others) who helped Billie's career at important stages in her life.

down segregation and discrimination, present good jazz and make bread for myself and the musicians as well. I felt that it made no kind of sense to treat a musician with any kind of dignity and respect onstage and then make him go around to the back door when he's offstage. I don't understand that treatment.' Roy Eldridge, who suffered badly from racial discrimination, says of Granz: '... he was the first to break down all that prejudice, he was the first to put the music up where it belongs. They should make a statue to that cat, and there's no one else in the business end of this business I would say that about.' As Whitney Balliett has observed, Norman Granz is widely regarded 'as the first person who has ever been able successfully to mass-produce jazz'. A pioneer in the staging of 'live' recordings, Granz was also one of the first producers to utilize the extended playing time of LP records. During the 1940s and 50s, JATP audiences (captured on record) were noted for their uninhibited responses to his concerts, whistling, cheering and stamping their feet with, Balliett suggests, 'a mass intensity that would have soothed Hitler, and frightened the pants off Benny Goodman'.

In 1952 Granz added Billie Holiday to his roster of recording artists, guaranteeing her a regular source of income. Under Granz's direction, Billie made a series of albums, generally of superior material, and with the support of first-rate accompanying groups. (See Discographical Essay.) Although Granz, along with many others, detected a gradual deterioration in Billie's voice as she began to drink more heavily, in 'The Long Night of Lady Day' he observed: 'I think that whatever qualities Billie had, like any artist, as the years go by, you have to use a different set of values.' He was, of course, also aware

Norman Granz's recording artist, 1950s.

that Billie was a heroin addict when he signed her for Verve records. Anita O'Day has reflected on the early 1950s: 'In those days, if you were a hype, most major record companies wouldn't have anything to do with you. But Norman built his label on junkies. In the bebop era it was hard to have a jazz label if you didn't deal with hypes. Norman had Charlie Parker, Billie Holiday, Lester Young, and most of the known users, including me.'

'Yet even the sympathetic Granz, whose father had lost his department store during the Depression, forcing the family to move from Long Beach to the less salubrious area of Boyle Heights, on at least one occasion expressed his anger at Billie's apparent urge for self-destruction. He rhetorically demanded of Leonard Feather: 'Why the hell should I sympathize because of her childhood? Mickey Cohen and I came from the same area in Boyle Heights. Mickey Cohen became a gangster; I didn't. Nobody forced him to become what he became.' Leonard Feather himself inclined towards the same view. Ruminating on Billie's fall from grace in 'The Long Night of Lady Day', he concluded: 'I think she was self-destructive because there were times when she could possibly have pulled herself out of the morass into which she had sunk. I think a lot of it had to do with the men she associated with and the kind of life that she led in general. Unfortunately, she didn't have enough self-control . . . There were times when she definitely was off drugs, and if she hadn't been around the wrong people she might have stayed off them.'

From the mid-1940s until her final collapse, Billie's public performances and studio dates were often erratic and always unpredictable, as she fought a series of losing battles with alcohol, drugs, and the unsavoury men she attracted—and was attracted to. These episodes were particularly distressing to those who had known her in happier times. Towards the end of her Decca contract, Milt Gabler recalls noticing that he was having great difficulty in getting the songs the way he had in the beginning. 'I would have to wait until her voice opened up. I would send out for a bottle of Napoleon brandy . . . and she would go into our Studio B and . . . in the interim, I would get everything rehearsed, all the arrangements, the band balanced, and she would come in from the other studio and we would get our four numbers in about forty-five minutes.' In *Jazz Voices*, Gabler adds the pertinent comment: 'The company never knew I was recording her in forty-five minutes when she was booked for three hours, and getting high on recording dates.'

Jazz writer and photographer William P. Gottlieb, who had seen and heard Billie in her prime, visited a 52nd Street club where she was appearing in 1949. His account of the occasion, in *The Golden Age of Jazz,* is a sad one: 'I arrived after eleven at night; and although Billie had been scheduled to start hours earlier, she had yet to appear onstage. In a way it didn't matter, for there were scarcely any customers. Word had spread that Billie's voice was shot, and that, anyway, she had become unreliable and might not show . . . I still hoped to get a story and a picture; so I snooped around the dressing rooms looking for Lady Day. I found her—alone, half-dressed, and too far out of it to get herself together. At least, not without help. I somehow managed to get her to the microphone. Then I wished I hadn't. I couldn't get myself to take notes. I couldn't get myself to take pictures. Lady had ten years left, and parts of them would be good. But that night on 52nd Street she seemed finished, and, in a sense, she was.'

Jack Schiffman, who helped his father run the Apollo Theatre, had an experience very similar to that of Gottlieb. In *Uptown* Schiffman relates: 'The last time I personally saw Billie was several years before her untimely death. She had a disturbing, exotic beauty that always reminded me of Gauguin's South Sea Islanders, but there was a somber melancholy in those dark eyes . . . It was as though she was getting a message from somewhere else and you weren't really there. Her diction was always slurred and muted as if she were drunk, but her intoxication was the otherworldliness of the addict. I walked into her dressing room that morning, apparently catching her on the heels of an altercation with the manager. There she stood, her dark, lustrous hair fairly glowing, her magnificent eyes staring from the depths of that fantastically boned face. She swayed back and forth muttering, "Oh, what a fool I am, what a goddamned fool!" I backed out of her dressing room, not wishing to intrude on such an intimate dialogue.'

In 1954, before she made her first European tour, Billie had another grim reminder of her Baltimore childhood. Unable to secure a passport because she could not produce a birth certificate, Billie returned to the Catholic institution where she had spent such a terrifying time, in order to obtain documentary evidence of her date and place of birth. The nightmares she had experienced in Alderson were literally revisited. She found the same Mother Superior still in command, saw the places where she had slept, been baptized and confirmed—and the place where she had been locked up with her dead companion. But, these painful memories notwithstanding, the visit produced tangible results—she was finally able to prove she was born in Baltimore and could now get a passport.

A musical romance: Billie and Lester in 1952, 'Laughing to Keep from Crying'?

Under the direction of Leonard Feather—'our M.C. and shepherd'—'Jazz Club USA' included, in addition to Billie, the pianist Beryl Booker, Carl Drinkard (Billie's accompanist on the tour), clarinetist Buddy De Franco, vibraphonist Red Norvo, and bassist Red Mitchell. As part of the troupe (which was recorded in Cologne), Billie performed in Sweden, Denmark, Germany, Belgium, Holland, France and Switzerland, as well as giving concerts in England as a solo artist.

Accompanied by her third husband, Louis McKay, Billie— as she recounts in her autobiography—was overwhelmed by her reception in Europe and Scandinavia and made many new friends. In London she was rescued from the unwelcome attentions of a journalist, concerned only with her drug addiction, by the critic Max Jones and was impressed to learn from him that in Britain the National Health Service treated addicts as patients. Billie soon warmed to Jones: 'I had never laid eyes on the man before . . . but he knew things about me that I'd forgotten and after a few minutes I felt like I'd known him all my life.' Jones, who met Billie at London airport, recalled for *The Wire* in 1984: 'I saw an imposing woman of average height . . . with handsome, well-boned features and an intolerant faintly mocking expression . . . Her speaking voice was slurry, a little cracked in tone . . . What she said inclined to the brief, hip and pithy. She had dignity and natural magnetism . . . an odd amalgamation of naivety and experience.'

Billie opened her short British tour at the Free Trade Hall in Manchester on 12 February 1954. Reviewing the concert for the *Melody Maker,* Jones reported: 'On stage, she looks calm and dignified, but she also looks warm, and sounds warm, and her whole attitude seems spontaneous and very, very hip.' (When the sound system failed at Manchester, Billie sang *My Man,* without amplification, to a delighted audience.)

In London Billie appeared at the Royal Albert Hall with Jack Parnell's orchestra and sang fiteen songs—ending with *Strange Fruit*—for a capacity crowd. Billie remembered the night of her big concert in London as the greatest thrill of her life. She was particularly impressed with the audience which she considered far superior to their New York equivalent. 'After I was introduced you could have heard a pin drop in that huge place. You could hear my heels clicking as I walked to the centre of the stage.' After her performance, this respectful silence was replaced by thunderous applause.

The singer Yolande Bavan believed that Billie, despite, or perhaps because of her rapturous receptions in England, was very lonely, possibly because so many people idolized her and felt slightly inhibited by the aura she presented. But to Bavan herself, as with so many other female performers, Billie was 'very maternal'.

In spite of a hectic schedule, missed planes, missing luggage, and the discovery of a hypodermic syringe in her dressing room in Stockholm—which may well have been dropped by a visiting Swedish musician—as Feather reported to the *Melody Maker* on 23 January 1954, half-way through the tour 'Billie was looking and singing better than she has in years. She has been

London airport, 1954: Billie with Carl Drinkard and Taps Miller.

bringing out songs like *Strange Fruit, Don't Explain, My Man,* and *Porgy,* and it's a thrill to hear this unique voice back at the pinnacle of its form.' Not only was Billie singing well, her on and off-stage behaviour reflected her sense of well-being and exhilaration. Feather recalls that he was not surprised by her cooperation and deportment which, he felt, stemmed from the sharp contrast with her American experiences. The second-rate theatres, tawdry dressing rooms and inferior night clubs 'that typified her directionless career' in the United States, were replaced by audiences 'teeming with fans who had dreamed for years of seeing her'. The bouquets, courtesy and complete absence of racism or paternalism, boosted her morale. 'When treated like a lady, she acted accordingly.'

Back in America, Billie's morale was further bolstered by the publication of *Lady Sings the Blues,* and her 1956 Carnegie Hall Concert (recorded by Norman Granz) during which Gilbert Millstein read extracts from the book. In a programme which included such favourites of her repertoire as *Please Don't Talk About Me When I'm Gone, I Love My Man, Fine and Mellow, What a Little Moonlight Can Do,* and *I Cover the Waterfront,* Billie received loving support from some of her old colleagues— Buck Clayton, Roy Eldridge and Coleman Hawkins. Nat Hentoff wrote of the proceedings in *down beat:* 'The audience was hers, greeting her and saying goodbye with heavy applause, and at one time the musicians, too, applauded. It was a night when Billie was on top, the best jazz singer alive.'

'Riffin' the Scotch'—with Betty Jones at the Albert Hall, 1954.

The following year American television viewers saw one of the finest jazz programmes ever screened. Produced for CBS by Nat Hentoff and Whitney Balliett, and narrated by John Crosby, as part of the Timex Company's 'Seven Lively Arts Series', 'The Sound of Jazz' featured, among others, Henry 'Red' Allen, Count Basie, Jimmy Rushing, Coleman Hawkins, Ben Webster, Vic Dickenson, Thelonious Monk, Pee Wee Russell, Jimmy Giuffre, Lester Young and Billie Holiday. Superbly filmed and staged—with the participating musicians dressed informally—'The Sound of Jazz' brought Billie and Lester together for a moving performance of *Fine and Mellow,* the highspot of an hour of enthralling music-making (now available on Pumpkin records in its entirety, and with generally superior performances to those rehearsal sessions released earlier). Billie, at first angry because of the decreed sartorial informality— 'I've just spent five hundred goddam dollars on a gown!'— appeared in a simple sweater and slacks. Nat Hentoff's description of Billie's reunion with Lester Young, in *Jazz Is,* deserves quotation at length. 'Perched on a high stool she faced a semicircle of musicians who were all standing—except one, Lester Young. Prez . . . was sick. He had been so weak during the run-throughs that most of his solos during the previous segment . . . had been split between Ben Webster and Coleman Hawkins. Now Prez was slumped in his chair, his eyes averted from Billie, whom he had not spoken to for some time . . . throughout the rehearsals they had ignored each other. Lady Day began to sing; and in the darkened control room the producer, the director, and the technical staff leaned forward . . . as the performance got under way, mumbling expletives of wonder. The song, which Billie had written, was one of the few blues in her repertory, and this time she was using it to speak not so much of trouble but rather of the bittersweet triumph of having survived . . . that afternoon she was in full control of the tart, penetrating, sinuously swinging instrument which was her voice. It was time for Prez's solo. Somehow he managed to stand up, and then he blew the sparest, purest, blues chorus I have ever heard. Billie, smiling, nodded to the beat, looked into Prez's eyes and he into hers. She was looking back, with the gentlest of regrets, at their past. Prez was remembering too. Whatever had blighted their relationship was forgotten in the communion of the music. Sitting in the control room, I felt tears, and saw tears on the faces of most of the others there. The rest of the programme was all right, but this had been its climax—the empirical soul of jazz.'

In her spoken introduction to *Fine and Mellow,* with the band playing quietly in the background, Billie explained: 'The blues to me is like being very sad, very sick, going to church, being very happy. There's happy blues and there's sad blues. I don't think I ever sang the same way twice. One night it's a little bit slower, next night it's a little bit brighter, just according to how I feel. Anything I do, it's part of my life.'

But Billie's condition and her health were declining almost as rapidly as Lester Young's. In July 1957 she appeared at the Newport Jazz Festival with Mal Waldron as her accompanist on piano, Joe Benjamin on bass, and her old friend, Jo Jones, on drums. Throughout, Billie sounded ill at ease and in unsure voice (on what was to be the last recording she made for Norman

Granz). In October 1958, six months before her death, she appeared at the first Monterey Jazz Festival and, in one sense, was barely able to rise to the occasion. Promoter Jimmy Lyons recounts: 'She had no idea where she was or what she was doing. I knew her condition, so I announced Gerry Mulligan and Buddy De Franco. I told them to stand very close to her, because she was going out to centre stage to sing. Well, the people fell apart because it really was Billie Holiday up there singing. She was dressed in a kind of tight-fitting short skirt. She was swaying from side to side. Buddy De Franco would push her back and she would lean the other way. The two of them kept her upright.'

Perhaps because of her physical state, Billie was well-received by the Monterey audience. Writing in *Jazz Journal*, Berta Wood noted: 'The tumultuous applause at the end of Billie's set, seemed no less than she used to receive in her greatest days.' The British jazz critic, Albert McCarthy, was also at Monterey, and reported: 'The support she gets from musicians of every school is touching ... The tragedy that is hers makes her

'Fine and Mellow'—Billie with Lester Young, Coleman Hawkins and Gerry Mulligan (CBS Sound of Jazz, 1957).

appearance almost unbearable for me these days—the whole agony is right in the open every time she sings.' Ralph Gleason remembered seeing Billie 'sitting stiffly in the lobby of the San Carlos Hotel' on the morning after her Monterey appearance. 'The jazz musicians tried to ignore her. Finally, in that hoarse whisper that could still (after thirty years of terrifying abuse) send shivers down your spine, she asked, "Where you boys going?" And when no one answered, she answered herself. "They got *me* openin' in Vegas tonight."'

In addition to Las Vegas, Billie played engagements in Florida, Honolulu, California and Philadelphia (where Mal Waldron became her regular accompanist) with varying degrees of success and failure. In *Jazz Voices,* Waldron remembers of this period that Billie's performances reflected her unstable temperament. 'When she wasn't feeling too well, we'd play mostly blues tunes. And when she was feeling very good, we'd play happy tunes. Because she only sang what she *felt*. What she felt like singing at the moment.'

The jazz critic Mort Goode, who was living in Hollywood in 1958, went to see Billie at the Avant-Garde club on Third Street. He had not heard her for two years and despite the 'unhappy ending' to the evening, was glad that he went since he would never see her again. He discovered: 'There wasn't much left to the voice then. But the hurt and emotion and style came through. At first. Somehow Billie got through the opening number. Forgot a few lyrics. Ad-libbed lines to fill out the song.

With friend and accompanist Mal Waldron.

Struggled to a conclusion. The second number was even worse. More forgetting. Less ability to relate to what she was doing . . . And then the introduction into the third tune. I haven't a thought about what song it was. Billie was strung out. It was taking total effect . . . Somehow she sounded like a record slowing down. The words became more undistinguishable. And then, as the little group played on, Billie just stood there. Blank. Struggling for her voice. For her memory. And the spotlight went out.'

In November 1958 Billie, now separated from Louis McKay, returned to Europe where she gave poorly-received performances at the Smeraldo Theatre in Milan, and at the Olympia Theatre in Paris. Billie's engagement at the Smeraldo lasted only one night after the audience booed her second-house performance. In Paris the *Melody Maker's* correspondent Henry Kahn, who interviewed her backstage at the Olympia, reported: 'Lady Day, or the Princess of Harlem, as they call her in France, looked tired. She sat drinking a glass of Vittel water, and in a meandering voice said, "Since my separation from my husband I do not want to stay in the States. I want to settle

Backstage in Paris with an appreciative Jimmy Rushing, 1958.

106

in Britain because I love the people. In Britain they do not just call me a singer, they call me an artist and I like that.'''

Billie stayed on for a time in Paris to work at the Mars Club on the Rue St Benoit. It was here that she was found by her old friend Hazel Scott, who later told *Ebony* magazine writer Charles L. Sanders that Billie had 'just been given a rough time by the French public because her voice couldn't do what they wanted it to do on stage of the Olympia Theatre' and had started 'singing in a little club for whatever percentage of the take she could get'. When Billie began to sing 'a real bitter blues', Hazel, with personal problems of her own, started to cry 'pretty loud'. Billie stopped singing. 'She backed me into a corner and in a cold, dry voice said something I'll never forget. She said, "No matter what the motherfuckers do to you, don't ever let them *see* you cry". That's the kind of person she was—always concerned about somebody else, always trying to protect the people she cared about. The tragedy was that she couldn't protect herself.'

Following her Mars Club engagement, Billie made a flying visit to London in February 1959 (with Mal Waldron, who had also accompanied her to Italy and France), where she appeared on the TV show 'Chelsea at Nine', backed for two of her numbers by the Peter Knight orchestra. Billie was visibly ill and ill-at-ease, and after the session said: 'I was so nervous out there, at first I could have died. Everything is a little different from American TV. I do hope that people like it.' Beryl Bryden, the British singer who had been introduced to Billie by Mary Lou Williams in Paris during the 1954 tour, recalled for Kitty Grime that she had taken some photographs 'of her the last time she was in London, the year she died. She looked very, very beautiful, but she was painfully thin. You could see she was really quite a big lady who'd shrunk. She had that lovely smile and she could get it together for the show, but when she was relaxed, all the sadness shows. I won't have those sad pictures published.'

On 15 March 1959 Lester Young, who had completed a recording session in Paris only two weeks earlier, died of a heart attack in a New York hotel. In his last interview, given to the journalist Francois Postif, Lester—already chronically sick—was asked: 'You've known Billie for a long time, haven't you?' His reply was simple and direct. 'When I first came to New York I lived with Billie. She was teaching me about the city, which way to go, you know? She's still my Lady Day.'

Many critics, as well as some musicians, have seen striking artistic and personal similarities in the careers of Lester Young and Billie Holiday. The pianist Dave Frishberg summed up this point of view for *Jazz Voices*. 'I think of Billie Holiday and Lester Young in tandem . . . if you look at their recorded output, and the pattern and shape of their lives, they paralleled each other, right downhill . . . The greatest product they ever turned out was in the beginning. And then their tones changed in kind . . . went from bright, rhythmic and vital, to dead, deadpan, maudlin. Billie's singing at the end sounds just like Lester's playing at the end. And vice versa. It's as if the two of them were bit by the same bug and went down together.'

Leonard Feather, who escorted a grief-stricken Billie to Lester's funeral, saw her slip a small bottle of gin into her purse as they left the service. Billie hoped to sing at the funeral, but wasn't asked. As Dan Morgenstern noted in the *Jazz Journal:* 'The family wanted a respectable funeral.' When the proceedings were over, Billie confided to Feather, 'I'll be the next to go.'

One of her other white mentors, John Hammond, has his own memory of the occasion. 'After the service I went down in the elevator with Billie. I think she realized that part of her own life ended with Lester's death. They were an odd, aloof pair, not much at ease in this world, and they found much comfort in each other's company . . . There had been estrangement, too, but a quiet reconciliation before the end. Within a month of Prez's death she was gone too.'

Appearing on British TV, February 1959: 'Chelsea at Nine'.

CHAPTER 5

BODY AND SOUL

'All dope can do is kill you—and kill you that long slow hard way. And it can kill the people you love right along with you.'

Billie Holiday

'Doctors have told Billie Holiday to give up liquor or it will only be a matter of time.'

down beat, 11 June 1959

On 25 May 1959, after an unsuccessful engagement at a small club in Lowell, Massachusetts, Billie Holiday made what was to be her last public appearance, a benefit concert at the Phoenix Theatre in Greenwich Village. Leonard Feather, who shared with Steve Allen the role of master-of-ceremonies, describes Billie's condition just before the show: 'I looked into her dressing room to say hello, and saw her seated at the make-up table coughing, spittle running unchecked down her chin. Looking at her, I was on the verge of tears and she knew it. "What's the matter, Leonard? You seen a ghost or something?" Indeed I had . . . she had lost at least twenty pounds in the few weeks since I had last seen her.'

Barely able to walk to a conveniently placed microphone, Billie managed to get through *'T'Ain't Nobody's Business If I Do,* and then had to be helped from the stage. Despite the urging of Feather, Joe Glaser and Allan Morrison, New York editor of *Ebony,* Billie refused to go to hospital. Six days later she collapsed in her apartment and went into a coma. A police ambulance took her to the private Knickerbocker Hospital, where, after an hour's wait, she was said to be suffering from 'drug addiction and alcoholism'. Billie was then transferred to the Metropolitan Hospital in Harlem, where she was registered as Eleanora McKay. In 'The Long Night of Lady Day', Metropolitan's Dr Kurt Altman remembered that Billie was in a very serious condition—emaciated, prematurely aged, and suffering from cardiac and respiratory problems. Examining her skin, 'we noticed several leg ulcers, secondary infective sites, where injections had taken place in the past'. But in the opinion of her personal physician, Dr Eric Kaminer, after he arrived on the scene, Billie's illness had no direct connection with narcotics. After three days, when Billie showed no withdrawal symptoms, the hospital confirmed Kaminer's opinion, and her condition was diagnosed as cirrhosis of the liver, complicated by heart failure.

For a time, Billie seemed to be recovering and received a steady stream of visitors, including her estranged husband Louis McKay (who flew in from California), William Dufty and his wife Maely, Mal Waldron, Joe Glaser, and her friend and attorney Earle Warren Zaidins, who had her moved from the public ward to a private room.

On 12 June, New York narcotics detectives searched Billie's hospital room and allegedly found an envelope containing heroin. She was charged with possession, arrested and, because she was too weak to be moved, placed under police guard. Whether or not the charge was true—and as Maely Dufty subsequently pointed out, it was unlikely that Billie, in her condition, could have reached let alone used the drug—it was a final humiliation. Alice Vrbsky, Billie's Czechoslovakian-born maid, secretary and companion for the last two years of her life, is certainly of this opinion. 'It was . . . like the last straw that the system could do to her . . . the arrest took a lot out of her . . . She couldn't believe they would do that to her.'

On 15 July 1959 Billie Holiday received the last rites of the Roman Catholic Church; she died two days later, in Room 6A12, at 3.10am. Elizabeth Hardwick writes: 'Billie died in misery from the erosions and poisons of her fervent, felonious narcoticism. The police were at the hospital bedside, vigilant lest she, in a coma, managed a last chemical inner migration.' When the hospital staff removed her body, they found that Billie—always a firm believer in hard currency—had $750 in fifty-dollar bills taped to one of her legs—an advance payment for a series of autobiographical articles.

Milt Hinton, the bass player (and accomplished amateur photographer) was one of the hundreds of jazz performers, friends and associates who attended Billie's funeral service at St Paul the Apostle Church on 21 July 1959. When the service ended, Hinton recalled that there was an awed silence among the assembled musicians, who filed out of the Church and stood quietly on the street corners. 'There was not the usual thing of musicians going to a bar after the guy has gone and having

110

a drink—a kind of New Orleans festivity. It was just dead quiet and sadness.'

Appropriately, it was Father Norman J. O'Connor, the Catholic chaplain of Boston University, and a staunch jazz enthusiast and broadcaster, who obtained permission for Billie to be buried close to her mother in St Raymond's Cemetery in the Bronx. (O'Connor receives an honourable mention in Billie's autobiography.)

Throughout her life Billie Holiday received (and, after her death, retained) the admiration, affection and respect of her peers. At times she also aroused their exasperation, concern and irritation. Warm in her friendships and sincerely solicitous of those she considered at risk, Billie, in her final illness before her admission to hospital, enjoyed the attentions of her friends on their visits to her apartment. Singer Annie Ross used to wash Billie's hair and 'bath her like a baby'; Alice Vrbsky was in constant attendance. A group of friends, including Annie Ross, William Dufty, Jo Jones and Leonard Feather, helped Billie celebrate her 44th—and last—birthday, three months before her collapse. (Feather reported that Billie looked stunning 'in leopard-skin blouse and skin-tight toreador pants'; Annie Ross remembers that Billie 'really sparkled' at her birthday party.) Among Billie's fellow musicians—and particularly among women—there was and is general agreement about her personality, if not the precise nature of her personal problems, exacerbated as they were by her addictions to alcohol and heroin. By turns, these friends and admirers found Billie kind and gentle, irascible and violent, happy and sad, the victim of racism and predatory men, self-pitying and irresponsible. Their assessments of her complex, volatile and troubled character need to be considered in any estimate of Billie Holiday, the artist and the woman.

Lena Horne, in her autobiography, states that Billie's life was essentially tragic, that she was corrupted by others—by white people and her own. Lena considered that Billie, insecure and confused, had nowhere to go except, finally, into 'that little private world of dope'. Her sensitivity and gentleness made survival, without the consolations of drink and drugs, impossible. Curiously, the two singers rarely talked about their

'Her animals were her only trusted friends . . .'

craft. In conversation, Lena remembers talking mainly about Billie's dogs—'her animals were her only trusted friends'.

But to Carmen McRae, reflecting on Billie's mishaps and misadventures even before her last illness, she was 'her own worst enemy'. Billie's troubles, Carmen believed, stemmed from an inherent unhappiness; singing was the only way she could express herself the way she wanted to be. 'The only time she's at ease and at rest with herself is when she sings . . . when she can sing, not when she's under the influence of liquor or whatever she's on. Lady is a very unpredictable person. Some nights people will listen to her sing and feel sorry for her, thinking she's through. Then the next night she sings her ass off . . .'

In a revealing interview, singer Sylvia Sims told *New Yorker* critic Whitney Balliett of Billie's impact on her—and of her own contributions to the Holiday image. Sims acknowledged Billie as her mentor—'I copied everything she did excluding the drugs and the booze'—dignified and beautiful, and possessing 'an innate sense of good taste'. This was reflected as much in the songs she sang as in her personal appearance. 'She was drawn to singing songs you know she understood. She had a kind of animal relativity to the songs she sang.' On one occasion, Sims presented Billie with a 'print gown' for her birthday, much to Billie's obvious delight. 'I can remember her in the gown at the Onyx Club, coming down those little stairs at the back . . . moving onto the stage and looking like a panther.' The dress was not Sims's only gift to Billie. 'She began wearing gardenias in her hair because of me. One night when she was working at Kelly's Stable, she burned her hair with a curling iron just before show time, and I ran down the street to the Three Deuces . . . Checkroom girls sold flowers then, and I bought a gardenia and Billie put it in her hair to hide the burned place.'

Hazel Scott, Billie's long-standing friend and disciple, felt strongly that the film *Lady Sings the Blues* conveyed a misleading and often distorted impression of her personality, problems and artistic temperament. Scott told Charles L. Sanders for *Ebony* magazine in 1973, following the successful release of the move: 'The thing I hope the kids don't miss—the ones who are just discovering Lady—is that she took a lot of the tragedy out of her life and made something beautiful out of it . . . She was always concerned about other people and very often she tried to bring to her music not sadness and despair but courage and love and the things you've got to have in order to cope . . . listen to her sing *Laughing at Life* and *Getting Some*

Fun Out of Life—and you'll know there were many dimensions to her, not merely the one of sad-faced junkie as so many people picture her.' Concerned only with box-office success, the makers of *Lady Sings the Blues* had, Scott believed, made a conscious decision to 'leave out all the beautiful things about her life ... They were fascinated by her addiction to narcotics and didn't seem to know that, except for a couple of highly-publicized arrrests, she handled that problem very, very well until the end of her life.' In *The Jazz Years: Earwitness to an Era*, Leonard Feather recalls that the movie was 'so flawed by inaccuracies and melodramatic cliches that Carmen McRae walked out of a screening before it was half finished.'

In the same article, Louis McKay, estranged from Billie at the time of her death, also disapproved, although on different grounds, of the depiction of Billie's drug addiction in *Lady Sings the Blues*—for which he received a percentage of the takings as 'technical advisor'. 'Neither the police nor the establishment,' McKay argued, 'mistreated her in any way. She was a 25- or 30-year narcotics user and they could have made things really tough for her if they'd wanted to. If people get an idea from the film that the feds and police harassed her, then that's wrong.'

McKay's judgment hardly seems to apply to Billie's final ritual humiliation in hospital yet, as she herself relates, during the war years when she was appearing on 52nd Street: '... every night they'd bring me the white gardenias and the white junk. When I was on, I was on, and nobody gave me any trouble. No cops, no treasury agents ... I got into trouble when I tried to get off.'

Taking issue with Hazel Scott, McKay maintains that the film did not present Billie in a negative way. In particular, McKay expressed satisfaction with the film's depiction of his relationship with Billie. 'I really like the way it shows the relationship she and I had. Billie and I were very much in love although we had our problems ... She was much, much more woman than most people realize who saw her only as a glamorous star, then as someone caught up in the narcotics thing. She was a tender, loving woman who liked nothing better than being at home with her man, cooking meals for me and doing little things around the house.' (Earle Zaidins remembers hiding Billie in one of the bathrooms in his apartment after she had been attacked by McKay—a scene not recreated for *Lady Sing the Blues*.)

Concerning Billie's musicianship, however, jazz performers and critics are in complete accord. To Anita O'Day, Billie remains 'the one true genius among jazz singers. She was unique. Only somebody who'd gone through the things she did and survived, could sing from the soul the way she did.' In *Jazz Voices* Carrie Smith considered that the way Billie sang 'was just totally in tune with her generation of jazz musicians'; Cleo Laine, a consummate singer in her own right, believes that 'Billie Holiday had a way of telling a story'; while for Beryl Bryden, although a lot of Billie's songs were of inferior quality 'she could find gold in them . . . She could make music out of talking'.

Ralph Gleason provides a graphic illustration of Bryden's last observation. 'I heard her say "baby" once, offstage and not in song . . . She had opened at a San Francisco night club and she was with her then manager John Levy . . . She had waited for Levy to come out of the club and had finally gotten into the car with a group of us. Then he arrived, slipped into the front seat, and she leaned forward and said, "Baaaaaaby, why did you *leave* me?" In that line was all the pathos of *My Man, Billie's Blues* and the rest. Nobody could say a word for minutes and she didn't even know what she had done.'

Nina Simone has remarked simply: 'As for Billie Holiday, every time I listen to her I hear more in the music than I heard before. I can't pay her a greater tribute than that.' Carmen McRae, who met Billie 'when I was in my teens' relates that: 'She really scared me as far as singing was concerned. She seemed so utterly perfect to me that I felt anything after her would be anticlimactic.' Betty Carter, a black singer who has herself refashioned and redefined the art of the jazz vocal, told Arthur Taylor: 'When you talk about a singer, you usually think about a pretty voice with a clear tone. Billie Holiday was a stylist with a particular and unique sound of her own . . . Her tone was unique, and what she did with her words was unique too . . . Billie Holiday had a sound and a way of approaching a song that was definitely hers.'

Billie's piano accompanists share a similar view. Like Johnny Guarnieri in the 1940s Bobby Tucker, a decade later, discovered that she was a joy to play for. '. . . with most singers you have to guide them and carry them along—they're either layin' back or else runnin' away from you. But not Billie Holiday. She had the greatest conception of a beat I ever heard. It just didn't matter what kind of song she was singin'. She could sing the fastest tune in the world or else something that was like a dirge, but you could take a metronome and she'd be right there. Hell! With Lady you could relax while you were playin' for her. You could damn near forget the tune.' Tucker also endorses a point made earlier by Carmen McRae, namely that Billie, always painfully aware of her inadequate formal education (her favourite reading matter was comic books) was less than articulate (and frequently obscene) in conversation. 'You could talk to her off the stand and hardly understand her, but when she sang, you could not only understand, you could *feel* what she meant.'

Interestingly, and perhaps not coincidentally, much the same thing was said about Billie's soul mate, Lester Young, who always spoke in a coded, colourful and idiosyncratic private language. The pianist Jimmy Rowles—who finally cracked the code—said: 'It was like memorizing a dictionary and I think it took me about three months.' One of Young's favourite phrases, used as an injunction to piano players, was: 'Just play vanilla man.' It meant, no embroidery or pyrotechnics, only supporting chords behind his solos. Whitney Balliett has provided some additional and priceless examples of Lester's argot. 'Bing and Bob' were police; an attractive young girl was a 'poundcake', while 'Starled doe, two o'clock' meant that an attractive girl with doelike eyes was in the right-hand side of the audience. 'I feel a draft' meant that Lester sensed the presence of a racial bigot. A 'grey boy' was a white man—Young himself, who was light-skinned, was an 'oxford grey'. 'Can madam burn?' meant 'Can your wife cook?' And 'those people who will be here in December' meant that his second child was due in that month. Although Lester named Billie 'Lady Day', her language, less esoteric than his, was equally forceful and uncompromising. Buck Clayton writes: 'Billie called all of her close friends MF. If she loved you she'd call you an MF—unless she was mad and then MF took on a more serious meaning . . . Billie must have loved me quite a bit because she called me an MF in almost every sentence.' Maya Angelou, on a shorter acquaintance, discovered that Billie's firmly-held opinions were delivered in a mixture of mockery and vulgarity, and that although she used common words: 'They were in new arrangements, and spoken in that casual tone which seemed to drag itself, rasping across the ears.' Billie had just returned from Honolulu, and when Angelou ventured to suggest that the Hawaiians were an attractive people, Billie snorted derisively: 'They just a bunch of niggers . . . running around with no clothes on. And that music shit they play. Uhn, Uhn,' and imitated the sound of a ukelele.

Mal Waldron, Billie's last regular accompanist, was impressed by the fact that her approach to a tune was that of a jazz musician. After hearing a new tune through several times on the piano, she instinctively formulated an overall approach and then 'She sang it as a *whole*. She didn't work on it bar by bar, the way most singers do. Jazz musicians think of a tune in terms of a unit, a sequence, how it moves; you have to, if you're going to solo on it. That's how she heard a tune . . . it was like playing for another horn. Because she responded to everything like a jazz musician.'

Max Kaminsky, who saw Billie at the Famous Door in 1936 and subsequently played for her in the Artie Shaw orchestra, offers a vivid description and informed analysis of her appearance and style. 'As a singer Billie had few physical mannerisms. She held her arms in the position of a runner ready to sprint, scarcely moving them except occasionally to snap her fingers in a lazy, leisurely movement . . . The basis of her phrasing was the beat, and she didn't distort the melody, but the stress and accent and meaning she gave the words somehow made the song larger than life-size. I've always felt the whole new form sprang complete in her mind with the first note she sang of any song. The art of improvising lies in the sense of structure, in the ability to build a new story out of the bricks and mortar of the original song . . . Billie was a master architect.'

Jazz vocalist, multi-instrumentalist and satirist Slim Gaillard had similar recollections of a typical Billie Holiday performance, as he recounted for *Jazz Voices*. 'She'd walk up to the microphone real slow, and she had one of the happiest smiles anybody could see . . . she'd just *melt* the audience with her personality . . . She just walked out there nice and slow, and she'd stand there and look. And smile. And then the piano or the group would wait until she'd say she was ready, and then she'd go into her song. She didn't do any of those cheap things singers do . . . she didn't need to. She just sang . . . She was *real* in front of an audience.'

Billie Holiday, then, presented popular (and not-so-popular) songs in person and on record in an inimitable style, to the delight of her admirers and the envy of her rivals. But what of the *content* of these songs? In common with many other female vocalists of her generation, Billie often conveyed sentiments calculated to anger present-day feminists, black and white.

In *Without Your Love* Billie says that, separated from her lover, she is like 'a song without words'/'a nest without birds'/'a violin without strings'/'a plane without wings'. But on his return, she feels 'on the crest of a wave'. And in *My Man* (one of her most-requested songs) Billie recounts: 'It cost me a lot, but there's one thing that I've got, it's my man.' And that 'Two of three girls has he, that he likes as well as me, but I love him.' Also 'When he takes me in his arms, the world is bright, all right,' so that 'What's the difference if I say I'll go away, I'll come back on my knees some day' since 'Whatever my man is, I'm his, for *ever* more.'

One response to such maudlin and self-disparaging lyrics is, of course, that (particularly in her early years) Billie had little control over the materials she recorded; that it is Billie Holiday the *singer,* and not the *song,* that demands critical appraisal—a point that will be taken up in a moment. But, and most tellingly, Billie herself (in collaboration with Arthur Herzog) made some notable contributions to this now suspect *genre.* In a 1956 radio interview with Tex McCleary and in answer to the question: 'Of all the things you've written, which one most nearly tells your story?', Billie unhesitatingly selected not one but two songs she had composed—*Don't Explain* and *Fine and Mellow.* McCleary then persuaded her to recite the lines of these songs like poetry, 'like a story'.

In her autobiography Billie recounts that *Don't Explain* came out of an episode in her marriage to Jimmy Monroe, who came home one night with lipstick all over his collar after being with a white English girl. Confronted by Billie, Monroe began to bluster, until she retorted bitterly, 'Don't explain.' The phrase stayed with her, other lines suggested theselves, and after collaboration with Arthur Herzog, the result was 'One song I couldn't sing without feeling every minute of it . . . Many a bitch has told me she broke up every time she heard it.'

More direct and earthy than *Don't Explain, Fine and Mellow*—an archetypal blues, and one of the few in Billie's repertoire—contains very similar sentiments, whether sung as a 'happy' or a 'sad' song.

In 'The Long Night of Lady Day', black feminist writer, Michele Wallace, with such lyrics in mind, asserts that feminists are justified in holding up Billie Holiday 'as a negative lesson to women . . . about how tragic a woman's life can be if she doesn't realize that her life is her own property'. But Wallace conceded, such a 'neat analysis' made her 'uncomfortable' for several reasons. Firstly, she had seen and heard Billie sing, and was also aware of her impact on the female members of her own family. Secondly, 'as a black woman, I know that she is my sister, in tears if not in blood.' The sentiments expressed by Billie in song ineluctably aroused in Wallace herself, as in other black women, 'immediate emotional and spiritual recognition'. Finally, Billie, however contrived her lyrics, spoke for all black women. 'There is an existential correctness about everything she ever said or sang, about being a woman.' Most significantly, Billie 'documented for all time the experience of *loss* that is so characteristic in a black woman's life'. Some of that loss she undoubtedly invited upon herself, 'but some of it just seeks you out and sweeps you up, and I can't deny that as a black woman'. 'Billie Holiday,' Ms Wallace concluded, 'paid too deeply for her expertise.'

The British critic and music historian Wilfrid Mellers makes the same point more succinctly—and without sole regard to colour. 'Billie Holiday's finest performances are those in which the irony is no more than latent in the understatement of passion . . . if the tune was good enough, and the words elemental enough, she could become every woman's representative.'

Yet in several respects, of course, Billie's adult experiences, like those of any other woman, regardless of class or colour, were unique. Her three marriages ended in failure and she had an unpleasant—and frequently violent—relationship with her lover/manager John Levy (a black man who was often 'mistaken' for white). Levy involved Billie in a narcotics charge in 1949 (on this occasion she was acquitted) and exploited her financially. In 1950 Levy, who had agreed to act as a backer for a tour of trumpeter Gerald Wilson's big band (featuring

Arriving at Stockholm Central Station, 1954. Carl Drinkard, Beryl Booker, Inez Cavanaugh, Billie, Leonard Feather.

Melba Liston) with Billie as vocalist, reneged on his promise and, as Billie recounts, 'walked out and left me with my goddamn band stranded in the Deep South without a dime'. Benny Morton suggested plausibly that: 'Very few of the men who were close to Billie were really interested in her . . . she was deceived by a lot of people, because any one could butter her up, saying nice things to her. She wanted to hear these things, because no grown-up seemed to love her when she was growing up.' Bobby Tucker recalls in *Jazz Voices* that when Billie was appearing at Club Ebony (during the time she was married to Jimmy Monroe) one of the owners 'just moved in and took her over. But it was all self-seeking. For *him* . . . she could pick 'em all right. She was attracted to that kind of person.'

In 'The Long Night of Lady Day', John Hammond states his belief that Billie 'didn't really have a very satisfactory sexual life'—possibly because of 'those early days in whore houses and loathing the kind of treatment she got there'. In the same programme, both Alice Vrbsky and Earle Zaidins express the opinion that Billie regretted never having children. Zaidins recalls that (at a time when she was not taking drugs) Billie was devastated when she was rejected as a prospective foster-parent by a child-adoption agency in Boston, because of her earlier narcotics conviction. Several of Billie's female friends, as has been seen, also referred to her strong maternal instincts. But Maya Angelou, who came to know Billie in California, only a few months before her death, remembers that at their first meeting Billie declared flatly: 'I can't stand children. The little crumb-crushers eat you out of house and home and never say "Dog, kiss my foot" . . . I can't stand the little bastards.' It is, of course, distinctly possible that Billie's feelings and responses towards children reflected her current state of mental and physical health. She appears, for example, to have been genuinely attracted to Angelou's son, Guy, criticized his mother for allowing him to wear ragged clothes, offered to buy him a new outfit, and attempted—without notable success—to modify her profane language when he was around.

Like her friends and contemporaries, who arrived at differing assessments of Billie's personality—none of them mutually exclusive—jazz critics have pointed to one or another of her personal and/or musical attributes in their attempts to define the true nature of her undoubted genius. There is general critical agreement that Billie was at her artistic peak in the 1930s and early 1940s, after which time alcohol, drugs and disillusion took their inevitable toll, with the 'later' Billie Holiday a pitful parody of her earlier self. Yet some dissenting opinions convincingly hold that there was no such decline from greatness—that the Billie Holiday of the 1950s (like Lester Young), despite ill-health, refined and distilled the essentials of her art and produced performances which, in their own right, stand as superlative artistic achievements.

Humphrey Lyttelton has made the interesting suggestion that a large part of Billie's disillusionment and bitterness—which saturate the pages of her autobiography—stemmed not only from racial discrimination but also from the fact that unlike her black contemporary, Ella Fitzgerald, who achieved over-night fame with her 1938 hit recording of *A-Tisket, A-Tasket,* she never had a similar success or won one of the jazz popularity polls in *down beat* or *Metronome.* (Billie did, however, win the first jazz poll conducted by *Esquire* magazine in 1944 and, ten years later, *down beat* presented her with a special award as 'one of the all-time great vocalists in jazz'.) Billie believed that her early records did not bring her adequate financial rewards, and recalled that from the more than two hundred sides made between 1933 and 1944 she received no royalties at all and was paid 'twenty-five, fifty, or a top of seventy-five bucks a side', and was glad to get it. (She did begin to receive royalties after her signings with Decca, Verve and Columbia.)

In 1946 Billie won a down beat *magazine award. Here she shows it to trombonist J. C. Higginbotham and trumpeter Henry 'Red' Allen at the Garrick Lounge in Chicago. The dog is Billie's Boxer 'Mister'.*

Despite her brutalizing experiences of racial (and sexual) discrimination, Billie Holiday—unlike, say, Nina Simone in a later period—was never a 'protest' singer. With the striking exception of *Strange Fruit,* Billie's work, as Lyttelton observes, lacks any specific social or political message. 'The sorrow, hurt, disillusionment and bitterness which lay close to the surface of her most light-hearted material may have originated, in part, from her racial circumstances, but the feelings conveyed through her huge recorded repertoire of bitter-sweet love songs are universal.' As a jazz singer *par excellence,* Billie Holiday both exemplified and transcended her racial identity—and this is, perhaps, the true mark of her creative genius. During the 1930s, when it was fashionable for black singers to sound 'white' in order to appeal to a wider audience, Billie remained a distinctively 'black' vocalist and never consciously adapted her intonation to suit popular tastes. This is the more remarkable when one considers her desire for popular acclaim, her lack of self-esteem, and the fragility of her ego.

Along with Bessie Smith, Billie's claim to recognition as the greatest of jazz singers is indisputable. Part of her artistic achievement was to create out of the lyrics of her songs—many of them excruciatingly trite and/or banal—the emotional intensity and profoundity of the blues. But, where Bessie Smith and the other 'classic' blues singers confronted and conveyed the pathos and despair in the lyrics they sang, Billie, denied access to the rich imagery of the blues as popular tastes began to change in the late 1930s, faced a formidable obstacle and one that could not always be resolved by making silly lyrics bear the weight of deeper meaning. Whitney Balliett observes of Billie's way with the lesser popular songs of her day: 'Her enunciation . . . was a mixture of clarity and caricature, bringing into action that rule of ridicule that the victim be reproduced perfectly before being destroyed . . . The composers of the pop songs she sang should be grateful; her renditions ("Ooooo-ooo-ooo/What a lil' moonlight can do-oo-oo") and not the songs, are what we remember.'

In this transformation of popular materials, and in the intimacy which she established with the listener, Billie Holiday had no counterpart in jazz. Charles Fox suggests that in these respects Billie, who 'always lived on edge of every song she sang', had her closest approximation in the French singer, Edith Piaf. But, as Ralph Gleason has remarked, Billie Holiday was something more than just a singer. 'She was a social message, a jazz instrumentalist, a creator whose performances could never be duplicated.' Although a whole generation of singers, whose inspiration she was, tried to emulate her style and inflections, 'None of them came any closer to it than sounding like Billie on a bad night.'

Given the undeniably slender resources of her vocal equipment—even in her early years—Billie's claim to be considered as one of the greatest jazz singers appears, at first, paradoxical. Henry Pleasants both recognizes and properly resolves this apparent paradox. 'Billie,' he observes, 'had to fit a song not only to herself, to her state of mind and body, and to an extraordinarily acute sense of style, but also to a meagre voice—small, hoarse at the bottom and thinly shrill at the top, with top and bottom never very far apart. She had hardly more than an octave and a third.' Yet, recognizing these physical limitations: 'What she achieved in terms of colour, shadings, nuances and articulation, and . . . the variety of sound and inflection she could summon from such slender resources, may be counted among the wonders of vocal history.' (Glenn Coulter once typified Billie's voice as 'clavichord-small and intense . . . of a monotonous colour that only the passage of time can vary'; during her last years, that distinctive voice deepened and 'darkened' considerably.)

Most critics (and some musicians) prefer Billie's earlier to her later recordings; Billie's own preferences were exactly the opposite. John S. Wilson, jazz reviewer for the *New York Times,* believes that by the 1950s, as her private life became increasingly difficult, Billie's voice and musical reflexes began to harden: '. . . like an ageing fast-ball pitcher who has lost his stuff, she was depending more on craft and guile to put across her songs . . . Through most of the Verve recordings . . . we hear a performer who is more diseuse than jazz singer, who is depending largely on mannerisms to carry her through tempos which are often killingly slow for a limited voice.' Whitney Balliett has written of Billie's 1950s recordings that she sang 'with a heavy, unsteady voice that sometimes gave the impression of being pushed painfully in front of her, like a medicine ball'.

One of Billie's last studio recording sessions (after she signed for Columbia)—"Lady in Satin"—on which she is accompanied by the Ray Ellis orchestra complete with strings and 'voices', is invariably cited by those who maintain that her later work was a travesty of what had gone before. John Chilton writes: 'The arrangements were not meant to be spectacular, they were to serve as a tasteful and unobtrusive background, one that would give Billie's harrassed voice a mellow accompaniment. Unfortunately, by the time of these recordings, Billie's voice is just not up to the scrutiny that the crystal-clear recordings provide. It's impossible to connect the sound of this crippled voice with the work of the young Billie Holiday. Billie said that she felt "Lady in Satin" . . . was one of the best records she ever made; that an artist of Lady's calibre should have thought this, indicates how troubled she was during the last part of her life.'

Writing in the *Jazz Review,* Glenn Coulter echoed Chilton's assessment of 'Lady in Satin': 'The name of a new Columbia record of twelve more or less insipid songs done by Billie Holiday against the neon arrangements of Ray Ellis.' Coulter judged the LP to be very nearly a 'total disaster' and continued: 'It is no pleasure to describe most of these performances, the gritty tone, the wavering pitch, the inability to control an instrument that is nothing without control; many times one can't name with any certainty the notes she is striving for. Billie's superiority ... has always rested in transcending her materials: hacking off melodic excess, and attacking the words with, alternately, deeper conviction and greater contempt. The ambiguity is, in her best performances, elusive and unpredictable, gives even rather foolish songs a startling resemblance to real existence ... Naturally, when sheer articulation becomes difficult, none of this can come into play. It does so in this set only once: *You've Changed* is remarkably free of flaws, and one is likely to play it over several times in delight without realizing how absurd the text is.'

Philip Larkin, noting the reissue of 'Lady in Satin' in 1968, wrote in *All What Jazz:* 'The sleeve claims that this reissue is in response to popular demand, but if so then popular taste is morbid, for this is in most respects a painful record. Billie's voice is like burnt paper, and does not sound fully under control: the lyrics of *For All We Know* are made by hindsight unbearably poignant.'

Statue—Billie Holiday.

It is, however, equally plausible to suggest that the undeniable deterioration in breath control, diction, and her always circumscribed vocal range—starkly evident on every track of 'Lady in Satin'—highlighted, as her earlier work had never done, Billie's uncanny ability to convey *meaning* in what had become an almost conversational tone. Drummer Max Roach asserts: 'I love "Lady in Satin". It told me a lot about her life, about her loves, her emotional ups and downs, what she had been through.' Singer Leon Thomas relates: 'I can listen to "Lady in Satin" and break into tears.'

Benny Green is one of the few critics who has argued that Billie's technical decline was of no real significance. 'In a way it only made her one supreme virtue more evident than ever. At the very end she was barely capable of singing at all in the conventional sense ... The trappings were stripped away, but, where the process would normally leave only the husk of a fine reputation, it only exposed to view ... the true core of her art, the handling of a lyric.' From this perspective, her last recordings are 'not the unsufferable croakings of a woman already half-dead, but recitatives whose dramatic intensity becomes unbearable, statements as frank and tragic as anything throughout the whole range of popular art.' In *Billie Holiday Remembered*, Martin Williams suggests that during the 1950s, although her voice may well have begun to fail and become 'disheveled', Billie, always a 'great dramatic performer', became 'an even greater jazz singer because she became a greater musician'.

From her unseasoned but joyous recording debut in 1933, through hundreds of subsequent recording sessions, countless night club performances, and scores of concert and theatre engagements, Billie Holiday was the authentic voice of jazz. From the poverty and intolerance of Baltimore and the squalor of a declining Harlem during the Depression, unstable family and marital situations, and the omnipresent and crushing reality of racial prejudice and discrimination, she emerged—perhaps because of these experiences—as a unique artist. In one of the most moving passages in her autobiography, Billie reflects: 'I've been told that nobody sings the word "hunger" like I do. Or the word "love". Maybe I remember what those words are all about.' She then goes on to assert a possible pride in wanting to remember the places and people from Baltimore to Hollywood that gave her her lumps and scars. But, 'All the Cadillacs and minks in the world—and I've had a few—can't make it up or make me forget it. All I've learned from all those people is wrapped up in those two words.'

At the present time, when drug addiction has become an issue of international concern, Billie's tortured, degrading and ultimately fatal embrace of narcotics should serve as an object lesson—if one is needed—to those who seek 'solutions' to their problems (real or imagined) in cocaine, crack or heroin. Billie, who never shook off her habit completely, declared three years before her death that drug addiction led not to 'kicks and thrills' but to physical and mental misery. And, echoing Charlie Parker, she asserted: 'If you think you need stuff to play music or sing, you're crazy . . . Dope never helped anybody sing better, or play music better, or do anything better. Take it from Lady Day. She took enough of it to know.'

But, if Billie Holiday never overcame her addictions to drugs and hard liquor, she did overcome that deeply-dyed prejudice which had for so long dictated that the proper place of a working-class black woman in America was either in the white woman's kitchen or in the clandestinely interracial brothel. In a male-dominated profession—that of the jazz performer and the jazz entrepreneur—Billie Holiday asserted the right of a black woman to an equal (in her case, a decidely superior) voice in the proceedings, both musical and financial. Not all of her encounters with men—black and white—were negative ones. White racial liberals and jazz enthusiasts (not a coincidental relationship) like John Hammond, Barney Josephson, Milt Gabler, Leonard Feather, Nat Hentoff, Ralph Gleason and Norman Granz played supportive roles in her career. As importantly, she also received encouragement, appreciation and

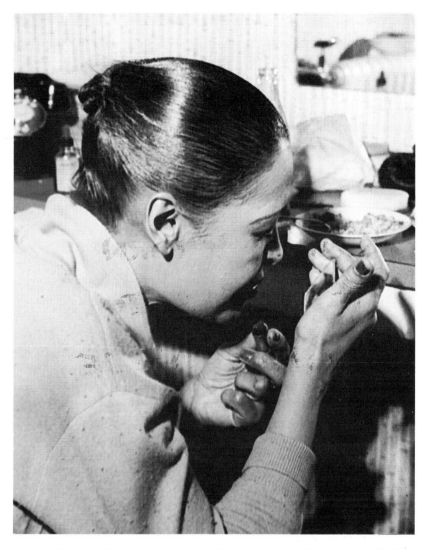

Preparing for her last appearance in England.

comradeship from such superlative jazz players as Teddy Wilson, Roy Eldridge, Johnny Hodges, Max Kaminsky, Artie Shaw, Benny Goodman, Bobby Tucker, Mal Waldron, Jimmy Rowles, Johnny Guarnieri, Frankie Newton, Ben Webster, Oscar Peterson, Benny Carter and, most rewardingly, her *alter ego*, Lester Young.

To a contemporaneous as to a later generation of women jazz singers and instrumentalists—Carmen McRae, Hazel Scott, Carrie Smith, Betty Carter, Nina Simone, Sylvia Sims, Anita O'Day, Annie Ross, Melba Liston, Beryl Bryden, Cleo Laine—Billie Holiday was the touchstone, the supreme exemplar of the esoteric art of the jazz vocal, the complete jazz musician, and a black beauty.

To a now ageing, but also to a younger generation of jazz

listeners, Billie Holiday remains, nearly thirty years after her death, as thrilling and vibrant as she was during her distinguished, anguished and tragically short life. Chris Albertson, in *Billie Holiday Remembered,* offers the sensitive reflection that: 'About the only thing left that is truly Billie Holiday's and which no one dares tamper with are the records which she made during the two-and-a-half decades of her turbulent career—records that preserve the nervous voice of a teenage girl making her debut among the giants of instrumental jazz, the spirited poignancy of her voice at its peak of maturity, and the pathos of the latter-day Billie whose voice, like delicate china of another time, showed signs of wear but retained its indefinable beauty.'

Belatedly, Billie was honoured in two cities which form part of her biography. Visitors to Baltimore can now view a statue of Lady Day set in a small open space among housing projects, on the corner of Pennsylvania and Lafayette Avenues, four blocks west from the black ghetto. Unveiled in 1981, by mayor (now Maryland Governor) William Donald Schaefer and 'The Citizens of Baltimore', Billie's monument was sponsored by the Committee for the Recognition of Black Contributions and—appropriately—the National Licensed Beverage Association. An accompanying notice and photograph of Billie contains a quotation from *Lady Sings the Blues:* 'I don't feel I'm singing. I feel like I'm playing a horn. I try to improvise . . . what comes out is what I feel.' And on 7 April 1986—on what would have been her 71st birthday—a 'Billie Holiday' star was placed in Hollywood's 'Walk of Fame', thanks to the unstinting efforts of Leonard Feather and the support of such performers as Carmen McRae, Jimmy Rowles, Artie Shaw, Jimmy Witherspoon, Dave Frishberg, Johnny Ray and Henry Mancini. Annie Ross said on this occasion: 'Every girl singer should get down on her knees and thank God there was a Billie Holiday.' With them, we should give thanks for Billie's life and cherish her real monument—those inimitable and irreplaceable recordings. Like Bessie Smith, Louis Armstrong, Duke Ellington, Benny Goodman, Count Basie, Lester Young, Teddy Wilson and Charlie Parker—and every creative artist—Lady Lives.

CHAPTER 6

FINE AND MELLOW
LADY DAY ON RECORD

Compiling a discography for any prolific recording artist is a specialized, thankless and ultimately self-defeating task, compounded equally of scholarship and antiquarianism. New issues and re-issues of the recordings of major jazz artists appear almost daily—only to be inexplicably withdrawn, amended or deleted within an equally short time. Again, in an age of 'budget' and 'nice price' (as well as imported) records and cassettes, old albums appear in partially or totally new guises—often with new titles and, invariably, minus details of recording dates and personnel. Additionally, compact discs are increasingly available. For these reasons, the recordings cited in this discographical essay are identified only by their original and/or current titles, and the labels on which they appear—record numbers have been omitted. Inevitably, some will only be available from the specialist jazz record shops, but the majority should be readily available.

In the case of Billie Holiday, Tony Middleton contributed a useful 'Selective Discography' to Burnett James's *Billie Holiday* (Kent: Spellmount, 1984), while *Lady Sings the Blues* (see Bibliography) contains both American and British discographies. Billie's recordings are also listed and discussed in the several jazz record reference books cited in the Bibliography.

The essential—and logical—starting points for appraising Billie's work are the major CBS collections: 'Billie Holiday: The Golden Years, Vol.1' (3 LPs) and 'Billie Holiday: The Golden Years, Vol.2' (3 LPs). Covering the seminal period from 1933 and 1942, these albums contain, among other treasures, Billie's first two recordings made with Benny Goodman: *Your Mother's-Son-in-Law* and *Riffin' the Scotch,* the Holiday-Wilson sessions, and air-shots with the Count Basie orchestra from the Savoy Ballroom, in 1937. Vol.1: Among other highlights in this volume are Billie's 1936 version of *These Foolish Things*, with superb accompaniment from Johnny Hodges on alto saxophone, *This Year's Kisses, A Fine Romance, I Must Have That Man, When You're Smiling, Without Your Love* and *I'll Never Be the Same*, all featuring the incomparable Lester Young on tenor saxophone. Roy Eldridge on trumpet provides particularly fine support for Billie on *I'm Pulling Through, Laughing at Life,*

Ghost of Yesterday, Time on My Hands and *Them There Eyes.* Whitney Balliett points out that Billie's 'simultaneous stretching and reshaping' of lyrics can be heard to particularly striking effect in 'the way she makes one long, bumpy word out of the first twelve words of *Them There Eyes* . . . "IfellinlovewithyouthefirsttimeIlookedinto—them there eyes"; once heard, never forgotten.'

If Vol.2 of 'The Golden Years' is not quite up to the peerless standards of Vol.1 (largely because of some of the inferior songs Billie was saddled with), there are still some rewarding performances to be heard among the forty-eight tracks: *Let's*

'. . . if the tune was good enough, and the words elemental enough, she could become every woman's representative.'—Wilfrid Mellers

Call the Whole Thing Off, and alternate takes of *Mean to Me* and *I'll Get By.* Less impressive are *It's The Same Old Story* and the appalling lyrics—beyond even Billie's powers of redemption—of *Mandy is Two.* Johnny Hodges is again heard to good effect on a stunning *You Let Me Down,* while Billie gives flawless renditions of *Moanin' Low, Carelessly, More Than You Know* and *Sugar*—the last two titles were recorded on 30 January 1939 and were the last sessions on which Teddy Wilson featured Billie as vocalist. Lester Young reappears on several items in Vol.2, including *Mean to Me* and *I Can't Believe That You're in Love With Me,* both of which also feature trumpeter Buck Clayton in fine form.

In every sense these two sets constitute the definitive pre-war Billie Holiday. They can be supplemented (and partially duplicated) by Vol.2 of 'The Lester Young Story: A Musical Romance' (2 LPs) on CBS, which contain such Holiday-Young collaborations as *When You're Smiling, Back in Your Own Backyard, If Dreams Come True* and *Now They Call it Swing.*

'God Bless the Child' (2 LPs) on CBS is a representative, if uneven, sampler of Billie's studio work between 1936 and 1942, twenty-eight sides, including her finest versions of *Gloomy Sunday, Georgia on My Mind* and *Solitude.* She can also be heard on the top of her form on several tracks of the CBS compilation 'Teddy Wilson and His All-Stars' (2 LPs)—a dazzling selection of Wilson small-group dates from 1936 to 1940. Billie's tracks include *With Thee I Swing, Things Are Looking Up, Who Loves You, These N' That N' Those* and the dreadful *Eeny Meeny Meiny Mo.* Ben Webster, Roy Eldridge, Bennie Morton, Buck Clayton and Johnny Hodges are among the supporting players.

Billie's Commodore/Decca period of the 1940s, when her vocal presentation became more mannered and her arrangements more elaborate, is well-represented on two albums: 'Billie Holiday: The Commodore Days, 1939-1944' (Ace of Hearts) and 'I'll Be Seeing You' (Commodore Classics). The first contains several takes of such standards as *I'll Be Seeing You, Embraceable You, He's Funny That Way* and *As Time Goes By.* The musicians on these tracks include Doc Cheatham, trumpet; Vic Dickenson, trombone; Eddie Haywood, piano; and Sid Catlett, drums. The second LP contains fine renditions of *Yesterdays, Fine and Mellow* and *I Gotta Right to Sing the Blues,* as well as Billie's first recording of *Strange Fruit.*

A selection of Billie Holiday recording sessions from the 1940s also appears on 'The Legend of Billie Holiday' (MCA), digitally remastered recordings with the orchestras of Toots Camarata, Bob Haggart and Bill Stegmeyer, and now also available on compact disc. Titles in this collection include *Lover Man, Don't Explain, Good Morning Heartache, My Man, Them There Eyes* and *God Bless the Child,* but the outstanding track is Billie's moving version of *Porgy,* accompanied by pianist Bobby Tucker.

Billie's contract with Norman Granz resulted in prolific series of studio and concert recordings, all of which are available on 'Billie Holiday: The Voice of Jazz,' Vols.1-10 on Verve. These are variable in quality but all rewarding, particularly when Billie is backed by such friends as Ben Webster, Harry Edison, Benny Carter, Charlie Shavers and Oscar Peterson, all of whom appear on Vols.7-9, recorded in January 1957. On these records Billie produces brilliant interpretations of such superior songs as *Day In, Day Out, Just One of Those Things, One For My Baby* and *Comes Love.* Vol.1 has Billie's 1946 JATP Los Angeles concert performance, including *Body and Soul, Strange Fruit, Travlin' Light, He's Funny That Way, The Man I Love* and *Billie's Blues;* her supporting group features Milt Raskin on piano, Joe Guy and Buck Clayton on trumpets; Willie Smith on alto saxophone; Lester Young and Red Callender. In their own right, these Verve recordings are as revealing and often as thrilling as her sessions of the 1930s and 1940s. Billie's famous 1956 Carnegie Hall concert—complete with readings from her autobiography—is also available separately on Verve, as is her 1957 Newport Jazz Festival appearance with Mal Waldron on piano; Joe Benjamin, bass; and Jo Jones, drums. 'The Billie Holiday Songbook' (Verve) is a well-chosen anthology of her Norman Granz recordings including *Good Morning Hearthache, Lady Sings the Blues, Don't Explain* and *Lover Man.* (The CD version of this album contains three additional tracks not included on the LP: *What A Little Moonlight Can Do* and *I Cried for you* (both featuring Charlie Shavers) and *I Cover the Waterfront,* from the 1956 Carnegie Hall Concert.) 'Billie Holiday: The Silver Collection' is a generous and excellent CD anthology of her small group sessions from 1956 and 1957, featuring Ben Webster, Harry Edison, Jimmy Rowles and Barney Kessel.

Billie's possibly inebriated (but certainly cheerful) engagement at the Storyville Club in Boston in 1951 is available under at least two different titles: 'Gallant Lady' (Monmouth-Evergreen) and 'A Rare "Live" Recording of Billie Holiday' (Recording Industries Corporation). Tenor saxophonist Stan Getz provides Billie with sympathetic and admiring support of *You're Driving Me Crazy,* while the remaining songs including *I Cover The Waterfront, Lover Man, Crazy He Calls Me, Strange Fruit, Miss Brown to You* and *All of Me,* have Billie accompanied by Buster Harding, piano; John Fields, bass; and Marquis Foster, drums. (The outstanding performance, however, is again Billie's rendition of *Porgy*).

'Lady Love' (United Artists) comes from a 1954 Cologne concert, in which Billie, accompanied by Carl Drinkard, Buddy De Franco, Red Norvo and others, produces husky, rhythmic deliveries of *What a Little Moonlight Can Do, Now Baby or Never* and an extended jam-session version of *Billie's Blues*. Of this last track, Whitney Balliett observes: *'Billie's Blues* is uncanny. Her voice by this time was half gone. It was full of boozy huskiness, her intonation was shaky, and her rhythmic deftness had slowed to a lumber . . . But in *Billie's Blues* she miraculously puts everything together again, and we hear the Billie Holiday of 1939. Her voice is smooth and her pitch perfect. Her phrasing has that languorous quality she gave the blues. And her feelings are unavoidably clear, just below the skin of the melody. It was an astonishing rejuvenation.' In the same year Billie appeared with the Count Basie orchestra at a Carnegie Hall concert. 'Live at Carnegie Hall: Various Artists' (2 LPs) on Roulette Records, has Billie in attacking form on *Lover Come Back to Me, Them There Eyes, 'Ain't Nobody's Business* and other songs.

Billie can also be heard briefly in a 1952 Carnegie Hall appearance—'Concert At Carnegie Hall' (2 LPs) on DJM Records—where she is introduced by Duke Ellington as 'one of the artists always imitated, with varying degrees of success . . . a symbol of good taste and good music', and sings *Lover Come Back to Me,* with Tony Scott on clarinet.

On 'Jazz at the Plaza' (Columbia) a 1958 'live' session, recorded at the Plaza Hotel in New York (which also features Duke Ellington's orchestra with Jimmy Rushing), Billie, accompanied by a tightly-muted Buck Clayton and a rhythm section, turns in creditable performances of *When Your Lover Has Gone* followed by her slow ballad, *Don't Explain*.

'Duke Ellington's Big Band Shorts 1929-1935' (Biograph) contains Billie's short vocal, based on *Saddest Tale,* from the picture *Symphony in Black*. 'Louis Armstrong/Billie Holiday' (Giants of Jazz) is the complete (previously unissued) musical soundtrack of the movie *New Orleans*. 'Billie Holiday: Songs and Conversations' (Paramount) is a collector's item: Billie talks, jokes, swears and sings her way through a Los Angeles rehearsal with pianist Jimmy Rowles and bassist Arthur Shapiro, shortly before her death. Rowles is in sparkling form throughout; Billie reminisces about her famous audition at Pod's and Jerry's, delivers some colourful anecdotes, sings

fragments of some songs, and two full versions (quite appropriately) of *Please Don't Talk About Me When I'm Gone*. A fascinating record. On 'For a Lady Named Billie' (Giants of Jazz) she can be heard in two extended radio interviews from 1956 and singing, among other numbers, *I Wonder Where Our Love Has Gone* and *Them There Eyes*. Her inebriated performance at the 1958 Monterey Jazz Festival can now be heard—and judged—on 'Billie Holiday at Monterey' (Black-Hawk Records), where she receives the musical (as well as physical) support of Gerry Mulligan, Buddy De Franco, and Benny Carter—with Mal Waldron on piano.

'Billie Holiday: Lady Sings the Blues' (Giants of Jazz)—one of several LPs with this title—is an excellent compilation and selection of her recordings from 1945 to 1957, including the title track (from the 1957 Newport Jazz Festival) and mid-1950s versions of *How Deep is the Ocean, What a Little Moonlight Can Do, Easy to Love, Too Marvellous for Words,* and *Nice Work If You Can Get It.* Charlie Shavers, Harry Edison, Benny Carter, Jimmy Rowles and Oscar Peterson are among the accompanying musicians.

'The Real Sound of Jazz' (Pumpkin) contains the complete soundtrack of the 1957 CBS broadcast, 'The Sound of Jazz,' and has as its prodigious climax Billie's re-union and 'reconciliation' with Lester Young on *Fine and Mellow*. On this track Billie also receives outstanding support from Coleman Hawkins, Ben Webster, Gerry Mulligan, Vic Dickenson and Roy Eldridge—who delivers a blistering and climactic solo.

'Lady in Satin' (CBS Cameo) is (as has been mentioned) the record that critics disagree so strongly about. It should be heard (and evaluated) by anyone interested in Billie Holiday's life and times—and is as essential a part of her *oeuvre* as the recordings of the 1930s. The outstanding tracks are *You've Changed, For All We Know,* and *I Get Along Without You Very Well.* Whatever one's personal reaction to this record it is, as one of its other song titles declares, *Easy to Remember (But So Hard to Forget).*

For Wilfrid Mellers, in his examination of *Angels Of The Night: Popular Female Singers of our Time*, Billie's 'painful and joyous integrity' shines through 'Lady in Satin'. In *The End of a Love Affair* 'she sounds, wasted by heroin, like an old woman; notes creak, croak and crack, and the rhythmic flexibilities seem often beyond her control.' Nevertheless, 'the emotional impact is considerable. The catch in the breath in the phrase "a little too fast", the *frisson* of fear on "fast", the wandering elongations on "stare" and "blare", the sudden efflorescence, followed by collapse, in the phrase "isn't really a smile at all''—such moments reassert the honesty that is the core of Billie's experience . . . Later Black women singers achieve marvels of expressivity as well as of virtuosity but cannot rival her unblinking veracity.'

Billie's final studio sessions, in March 1959—also with the Ray Ellis Orchestra—are available on 'Billie Holiday: Her Last Recording' (Jazz Magazine). Titles include: *All Of You, I'll Never Smile Again, Don't Worry 'Bout Me, Just One More Chance* and *Baby Won't You Please Come Home?* Billie, still in command of her impeccable timing and consummate rhythmic sense, is heard to advantage on *Sometimes I'm Happy* and *There'll Be Some Changes Made*. Harry Edison on trumpet and Gene Quill on alto saxophone, together with a rhythm section comprising Hank Jones, piano; Milt Hinton, bass; Barry Galbraith, guitar; and Osie Johnson, drums; provide sympathetic support. Sally-Ann Worsfold observed of this LP in *Jazz Journal International:* 'Obviously there is an abundance of much finer Holiday recordings, but as the final chapter of a largely tormented and tragic life this immensely moving album is far better than it has a right to be.'

Billie's Blues

BIBLIOGRAPHY

Angelou, Maya	*The Heart of a Woman* (New York: Random House, 1981)
Balliett, Whitney	*American Singers* (New York: Oxford UP, 1979)
	Dinosaurs in the Morning, (Philadelphia: Lippincott, 1962 and London: Phoenix House, 1964)
	Ecstasy at the Onion (New York: Bobbs Merrill, 1971)
	Such Sweet Thunder (New York: Bobb Merrill, 1966)
Basie, Count	*Good Morning Blues: The Autobiography of Count Basie As Told to Albert Murray* (New York: Random House and London: Heinemann, 1986)
Blesh, Rudi	*Shining Trumpets: A History of Jazz* (New York: Knopf and London: Cassell, 1958)
	Combo USA (Philadelphia: Chilton, 1971)
Buerkle, Jack V. and Danny Barker	*Bourbon Street Black* (New York and London: Oxford UP, 1973)
Cerulli, Dom, Burt Korall and Mort Nasatir	*The Jazz Word* (London: Dobson, 1963)
Chilton, John	*Billie's Blues* (London: Quartet Books, 1975)
Clarke, John H.	*Harlem USA* (Berlin: Seven Seas Publishers, 1964)
Clayton, Buck and Nancy Miller Elliott	*Buck Clayton's Jazz World* (London: Macmillan, 1986)
Colin, Sid	*The Life and Times of Ella Fitzgerald* (London: Elm Tree Books, 1986)
Cooke, Alistair	*The Vintage Mencken* (New York: Knopf, 1955)
Collier, James Lincoln	*Louis Armstrong* (London: Michael Joseph, 1984 and New York: Macmillan, 1985)
Crowther, Bruce and Mike Pinfold	*The Jazz Singers: From Ragtime to New Wave* (Poole, Dorset: Blandford Press, 1986)

Dahl, Linda

Stormy Weather: The Music and Lives of a Century of Jazz Women (New York: Pantheon Books, 1984)

Dance, Stanley

The World of Count Basie (New York: Scribner and London: Sidgwick and Jackson, 1980)

Ellison, Ralph

Shadow and Act (New York: Vintage Books, 1972)

Feather, Leonard

From Satchmo to Miles (London: Quartet Books, 1974)

The Jazz Years: Earwitness to an Era (London: Quartet Books, 1986)

Fox, Fred

Showtime at the Apollo (London: Quartet Books, 1985)

Gelly, Dave

Lester Young (Tunbridge Wells Kent: Spellmount, 1984)

Gillespie, Dizzy and Al Fraser

To Be Or Not to Bop (London: Quartet Books, 1982 and New York: Da Capo, 1985)

Gleason, Ralph J.

Celebrating the Duke, Louis, Bessie, Billie, Bird, Carmen, Miles, Dizzy, and Other Heroes (New York: Dell Publishing, 1975)

Gottlieb, William P.

The Golden Age of Jazz (New York: Simon and Schuster and London: Quartet Books, 1979)

Green, Benny

The Reluctant Art: The Growth of Jazz (London: MacGibbon and Kee, 1962)

Grime, Kitty

Jazz Voices (London: Quartet Books, 1983)

Hammond, John and Irving Townsend

John Hammond on Record: An Autobiography (London: Penguin Books, 1981)

Hardwick, Elizabeth

Sleepless Nights (New York: Random House and London: Weidenfeld and Nicholson, 1979)

Hentoff, Nat

Jazz Is (New York: Random House, 1976 and London: W. H. Allen, 1978)

The Jazz Life (New York: Dial Press, 1961 and London: Peter Davies, 1962)

Holiday, Billie and William Dufty — *Lady Sings the Blues* (Garden City, New York: Doubleday, 1956 and London: Penguin Books, 1984)

Horne, Lena and Richard Schickel — *Lena* (Garden City, New York: Doubleday, 1965 and London: Andre Deutsch, 1966)

Huggins, Nathan I. — *Harlem Renaissance* (New York: Oxford UP, 1971)

Hughes, Langston — *The Big Sea: An Autobiography* (New York: Hill & Wang, 1963 and London: Pluto Press, 1986)

Hughes, Spike — *Second Movement* (London: Museum Press, 1951)

Johnson, James W. — *Black Manhattan* (New York: Atheneum, 1968)

Jones, Max and John Chilton — *Louis: The Louis Armstrong Story* (Boston: Little Brown, 1971)

Kaminsky, Max and V. E. Hughes — *My Life in Jazz* (New York: Harper and Row and London: Andre Deutsch, 1963)

Kuehl, Linda, Ellie Schocket and Dan Morgenstern — *Billie Holiday Remembered* (New York Jazz Museum, 1973)

Larkin, Philip — *All What Jazz: A Record Diary 1961-1971)* (London: Faber, 1970)

Leab, Daniel J. — *From Sambo to Superspade: The Black Experience in Motion Pictures* (Boston: Houghton Mifflin, 1976)

Leonard, Neil — *Jazz and the White Americans: The Acceptance of a New Art Form* (Chicago: University of Chicago Press, 1962)

Levine, Lawrence W. — *Black Culture and Black Consciousness: Afro-American Folk Thought From Slavery to Freedom* (New York: Oxford UP, 1977)

Lyons, Jimmy and Ira Kamin — *Dizzy, Duke, The Count and Me: The Story of the Monterey Jazz Festival* (San Francisco: Hearst Corporation, 1978)

Lyttelton, Humphrey — *The Best of Jazz 2: Enter the Giants* (London: Robson Books, 1981)

Mellers, Wilfrid — *Music in a New Found Land* (London: Barrie and Rockcliffe, 1964

	Angels of the Night: Popular Female Singers of Our Time (Oxford: Basil Blackwell, 1986)
Mezzrow, Milton and Leonard Wolfe	*Really the Blues* (New York: Random House, 1946)
Newton, Francis	*The Jazz Scene* (London: Penguin Special, 1961)
O'Day, Anita and George Eells	*High Times Hard Times* (New York: Putnam, 1981 and London: Corgi Books, 1983)
Osofsky, Gilbert	*Harlem: The Making of a Ghetto* (New York: Harper and Row, 1968)
Ottley, Roi	*New World A-Coming: Inside Black America* (New York: Arno Press and *New York Times,* 1969)
Placksin, Sally	*American Women in Jazz 1900 to the Present: Their Words, Lives, and Music* (New York: Wideview Books, 1982)
Pleasants, Henry	*The Great American Popular Singers* (New York: Simon and Schuster, 1974)
Schiffman, Jack	*Uptown: The Story of Harlem's Apollo Theatre* (New York: Cowles Book Co, 1971)
Shapiro, Nat and Nat Hentoff	*Hear Me Talkin' to Ya': The Story of Jazz by the Men Who Made It* (New York: Rinehart and London: Peter Davis, 1955)
Shaw, Arnold	*52nd Street: The Street of Jazz* (New York: Da Capo Press, 1977)
Simon, George T.	*The Big Bands* (New York: Macmillan, 1971 and London: Collier Macmillan, 1974)
Smith, Charles Edward	*The Jazz Record Book* (New York: Smith and Durrell, 1944)
Smith, Willie 'The Lion' and George Hoefer	*Music on My Mind: The Memoirs of an American Pianist* (Garden City, New York: Doubleday, 1964 and London: The Jazz Book Club, 1966)
Stearns, Marshall	*The Story of Jazz* (New York: Oxford UP, 1970)

Taylor, Arthur	*Notes and Tones: Musician-to-Musician Interviews* (New York: Coward, McCann & Geoghegan, 1982 and London: Quartet Books, 1983)
Waters, Ethel and Charles Samuels	*His Eye Is On The Sparrow* (Garden City, New York: Doubleday and London: W. H. Allen, 1951)
Williams, Martin	*Jazz Panorama* (New York: Crowell, 1964 and London: Jazz Book Club, 1965)
	The Art of Jazz (New York: Oxford UP, 1959)
Wilson, John S.	*The Collector's Jazz: Traditional and Swing* (New York: Lippincott, 1958)

SUGGESTED READING

Albertson, Chris	*Bessie* (London: Sphere Books, 1975)
Anderson, Jervis	*Harlem: The Great Black Way* (New York: Farrar, Straus and Giroux and London: Orbis Publishing, 1982)
Balliett, Whitney	*New York Notes: A Journal of Jazz in the Seventies* (Boston: Houghton Mifflin, 1976)
	Night Creature: A Journal of Jazz 1975-1980 (New York: Oxford UP, 1981)
	The Sound of Surprise (New York: Dutton and London: William Kimber, 1959)
Callcott, Mary Law	*The Negro in Maryland Politics 1870-1912* (Baltimore: John Hopkins UP, 1969)
Case, Brian and Stan Britt	*The Illustrated Encyclopedia of Jazz* (London: Salamander Books, 1978)
Collier, James Lincoln	*The Making of Jazz: A Comprehensive History* (New York: Dell, 1979 and London: Macmillan, 1981)
Condon, Eddie and Richard Gehman	*Eddie Condon's Treasury of Jazz* (New York: Dial Press 1956 and London: Peter Davies, 1957)

Cripps, Thomas   *Slow Fade to Black: The Negro in American Film 1900-1942* (New York: Oxford UP, 1977)

Feather, Leonard   *The Encyclopedia of Jazz* (New York: Horizon Press and London: Arthur Barker, 1960)

Green Benny   *Drums in My Ears* (London: Davis-Poynter, 1973)

Gutman, Herbert G.   *The Black Family in Slavery and Freedom 1750-1925* (New York: Vintage Books, 1977)

Harrison, Max, Charles Fox and Eric Thacker   *The Essential Jazz Records Vol.1: Ragtime to Swing* (London: Mansell Publishing, 1984)

Haskins, Jim   *The Cotton Club* (London: Robson Books, 1985)

Hooks, Bell   *Ain't I a Woman: Black Women and Feminism* (Boston, Mass: South End Press, 1981)

Jones, Jacqueline   *Labor of Love, Labor of Sorrow: Black Women, Work and the Family from Slavery to the Present* (New York: Basic Books, 1985)

Lewis, David L.   *When Harlem Was in Vogue* (New York: Knopf, 1981)

McCarthy, Albert, Alun Morgan, Paul Oliver and Max Harrison   *Jazz on Record: A Critical Guide to the First 50 Years* (London: Talisman Books, 1977)

Oliver, Paul   *Screening the Blues: Aspects of the Blues Tradition* (London: Cassell, 1968)

Ostransky, Leroy   *Jazz City: The Impact of Our Cities on the Development of Jazz* (Englewood Cliffs, New Jersey: Prentice Hall, 1978)

Scheiner, Seth M.   *Negro Mecca: A History of the Negro in New York City 1865-1920* (New York: New York UP, 1965)

Shapiro, Nat and Nat Hentoff   *The Jazz Makers* (New York: Rinehart, 1957 and London: Peter Davies, 1958)

Southern, Eileen   *The Music of Black Americans* (New York: W. W. Norton, 1971)

Wells, Dicky and Stanley Dance	*The Night People: Reminiscences of a Jazzman* (London: Robert Hale, 1971)		
White, John	*Black Leadership in America 1895-1968* (London: Longman, 1985)		
Williams, Martin	*The Jazz Tradition* (New York: Oxford UP, 1983)		

NEWSPAPERS AND MAGAZINES

The newspapers and magazines used in this study are generally noted in the text. They include: *The Amsterdam News; The Baltimore Afro-American; Current History; down beat; Ebony; Essence; Jazz Journal International; The Jazz Review; The Ladies Home Journal; Metronome; The Melody Maker; The New Yorker; The New York Times; The Pittsburgh Courier* and *The Wire.*

INDEX

A-Tisket, A-Tasket 121
Albertson, Chris *32, 42, 128*
Alexander, Willard *48, 68*
All of Me 132
All of You 135
Allen, Henry 'Red' *102*
Allen, Jean *93*
Allen, Lewis (Abel Meeropol) *49–50*
Allen, Steve *74, 109*
Altman, Dr. Kurt *109*
Ammons, Albert *32*
Anderson, Eddie *81*
Angelou, Maya *11, 56, 116, 121*
Any Old Time 73
Armstrong, Louis *18, 22, 58, 80, 82, 86–87*
As Time Goes By 131

Baby Won't You Please Come Home? 135
Back in Your Own Backyard 131
Baker, Chet *85*
Balliett, Whitney *39, 48, 63, 75, 76, 96, 102, 113, 116, 123, 124, 130, 133*
Baraka, Imamu Amiri (Le

Roi Jones) *7*
Barker, Danny *84, 86*
Bigard, Barney *82*
Barnet, Charlie *71*
Basie, Count *32, 40, 65–68, 102*
Baskette, James *80*
Bastone, Frank *35*
Bavan, Yolande *100*
Bechet, Sidney *32*
Beiderbecke, Leon 'Bix' *85*
Benjamin, Joe *103*
Berg, Billy *78, 94–95*
Best, John *69*
Bigard, Barney *82*
Billie's Blues (Chilton) *12*
Billie's Blues 132, 133
'Black and White Minstrel Show, The' *79*
Blake, Eubie *22*
Blesh, Rudi *53–55*
Body and Soul 29, 132
Booker, Beryl *99*
Brit, Stan *64*
Brown, Claude *11*
Bryden, Beryl *107, 115*
Buerkle, Jack *85–86*

Cabin in the Sky (1943) *80*
Callender, Red *82, 95, 132*

Camarata, Toots *131*
Capehart, Homer *37*
Carelessly 131
Carney, Harry *39*
Carter, Benny *127, 132, 134*
Carter, Betty *7, 115, 134*
Catlett, Big Sid *51, 131*
Chant of the Weed 85
Cheatham, Doc *131*
'Chelsea at Nine' (1959) *107*
Chilton, John *12, 39, 65, 69, 86, 124*
Christian, Charlie *61*
Clay, Shirley *36*
Clayton, Buck *39, 40, 42, 101, 116, 131, 133*
Cohen, Mickey *97*
Cole, Cozy *36, 39*
Cole, Nat 'King' *95*
Collier, James Lincoln *86*
Comes Love 132
Condon, Eddie *42*
Conover, Willis *36*
Cooper, Ralph *43, 45*
Cordova, Arturo *82*
Coulter, Glenn *124*
Crain, Jeanne *81*
Crazy He Calls Me 132

Crosby, John *102*
Crowther, Bruce *76*
Cullen, Countee *12, 22*

Dahl, Linda *63*
Dance, Stanley *42, 64*
Daniels, Billy *78*
Davis, Angela *11*
Day In, Day Out 132
Dean, Alice *18*
De Franco, Buddy *99, 104, 133, 134*
DeMichael, Don *39*
Dexter, Dave *72*
Dickenson, Vic *102, 131, 134*
Dixon, Dave *82*
Dixon, William R. *28–29*
Don't Explain 118
Don't Worry 'bout Me 135
Dove, Billie *78*
Drinkard, Carl *99, 133*
Du Bois, W.E.B. *22, 58*
Duchin, Eddy *38*
Dudley, Bessie *46*
Dufty, Maely *110*
Dufty, William *10, 11, 110, 111*
Duke is Tops, The (1938) 81

Dylan, Bob *32*

Easy to Remember 134
Edison, Harry 'Sweets' *42, 95, 132, 135*
Eeny Meeny Meiny Mo 131
Eisenhower, Dwight D. *87*
Eldridge, Roy *36, 39, 71, 95, 96, 101, 127, 130, 134*
Ellington, Duke *22, 45, 133*
Ellis, Ray *124, 134*
Ellison, Ralph *61–62*
Emancipation Proclamation (1863) *10*
Embraceable You 131
End of a Love Affair, The 134
Esman, Harold *25*

Fagan, Charles *17*
Fagan, Sadie *10, 17, 19, 84*
Feather, Leonard *19, 57, 68, 72, 73–74, 82–83, 89–90, 93, 99, 100–101, 108, 109, 111, 114, 126, 128*
Fields, John *133*
Fine and Mellow 52–53, 101, 102–103, 118, 134
Fine Romance, A 130
Fitzgerald, Ella *19, 43, 95, 121*
For All We Know 125
Forrest, Helen *69*
Foster, Marquis *133*
Foster, Pops *60*
Fox, Charles *123*
Fox, Ed *47*
Fox, Ted *43*
Franklin, Aretha *32*
Frishberg, Dave *108, 128*
Furie, Sidney J. *10*

Gable, Clark *78*
Gabler, Milt *52, 97, 126*
Gaillard, Slim *117*
Galbraith, Barry *135*
Garvey, Marcus *21*
Gelly, Dave *40*
Georgia on My Mind 131
Getting Some Fun Out of Life 113
Getz, Stan *85, 95*
Ghost of Yesterday 39, 130
Gillespie, Dizzy *63, 95*
Gimme a Pigfoot 86
Giuffre, Jimmy *102*
Glaser, Joe *46–47, 84, 91, 109*
Gleason, Ralph J. *56, 105, 115, 123, 126*
Gloomy Sunday 131
God Bless the Child 28, 132

Golden Leaf Strut 85
Gone With the Wind (1939) 79
Goodman, Benny *32, 35–36, 43, 48, 54, 127*
Good Morning Heartache 132
Goode, Mort *105–106*
Gottlieb, William P. *97–98*
Grable, Betty *81*
Granz, Norman *78, 94–97, 101, 126, 132*
Green, Benny *9, 125*
Green, Freddie *65*
Gregory, Dick *11*
Grey, Harry *38*
Grime, Kitty *48, 50, 107*
Guarnieri, Johnny *76, 127*
Guy, Joe *84, 91*

Haggart, Bob *131*
Haley, Alex *11, 17*
Hall, Bob *35*
Hall, Edmond *71*
Hammond, John Henry *7, 31–39, 40, 46, 48, 65, 68, 86, 108, 121, 126*
Hampton, Lionel *43*
Handy, W.C. *22*
Harding, Buster *133*
Hardwick, Elizabeth *78, 110*
Harlem Air Shaft 25–26
Hawkins, Coleman *40, 95, 101, 102*
Haywood, Eddie *131*
Henderson, Fletcher *17, 22, 25, 29, 32, 47*
Hentoff, Nat *19, 39, 88, 89, 101, 102, 103, 126*
He's Funny That Way 131
Herman, Woody *82*
Herzog, Arthur *118*
Minton, Milt *110, 135*
Hironimus, Helen *93*
Hodges, Johnny *39, 127, 130, 131*
Holiday, Clarence *17, 29, 51–52*
Holiday, Sadie (see Fagan, Sadie)
Hollingsworth, Charles *29*
Hopkins, Claude *71*
Horne, Lena *48, 60–61, 71, 78–79, 81, 112–113*
Hot Time in the Old Town Tonight, A 82
House I live in, The (1945) 50
How Deep Is the Ocean 134
Huggins, Nathan *22*
Hughes, Langston *22, 24, 28*

Huges, Spike *31*
Humes, Helen *63–64*
Hurst, Fannie *60*
Hurston, Zora Neale *60*

I Can't Believe That You're in Love With Me 131
I Can't Get Started 66
I Cover the Waterfront 101
I Cried for You 39, 43
Idaho, Berta *13*
If Dreams Come True 40, 131
If the Moon Turns Green 45
I Get Along Without You Very Well 134
I 'Gotta Right to Sing the Blues 131
I Love My Man 101
I Wonder Where Our Love Has Gone 134
I'll Be Seeing You 131
I'll Get By 131
I'll Never Be the Same 40, 130
I'll Never Smile Again 135
I'm Pulling Through 39, 130
I Must Have That Man 40, 130
I Wished on the Moon 36
It's the Same Old Story 131

Jacquet, Illinois *95*
James, Burnett *129*
Jammin' The Blues (1944) 95
Jazz At The Philharmonic (JATP) *95–96, 132*
Jeremy, John *18*
Johnson, Bunk *82*
Johnson, James P. *32, 60*
Johnson, James Weldon *21–22*
Johnson, Jay Jay *95*
Johnson, Pete *32*
Jones, Hank *135*
Jones, Jo *39–40, 42, 43, 95, 103, 111*
Jones, Jonah *39*
Jones, Max and Betty *86, 100*
Josephson, Barney *48–50, 78, 126*
Just One More Chance 135
Just One of Those Things 132

Kahn, Henry *106–107*
Kaminer, Dr. Eric *110*
Kaminsky, Max *42, 68–69, 117, 127*

Kessel, Barney *132*
Key Largo (1948) 94
King, Dr. Martin Luther *71*
Kirby, John *39*
Knight, Peter *107*
Kramer, Gary *87–88*
Krupa, Gene *36, 64*
Kyser, Kay *38*

Lady in Satin 124–125, 134
Lady Sings the Blues (1972) 10, 113–114
Lady Sing the Blues (Holiday/Dufty) *9, 11, 101*
Lanchester, Elsa *35*
Laine, Cleo *115, 127*
Lang, Fritz *81*
Larkin, Philip *125*
Laughing at Life 113, 130
Laughton, Charles *35*
Leab, Daniel J. *81*
Let's Call the Whole Thing Off 131
Levy, John *115, 119–120*
Levey, Jules *81*
Lewis, Meade Lux *32*
Lindbergh, Charles *26*
Lincoln, Abbey *7*
Liston, Melba *63, 120, 127*
'Long Night of Lady Day' (BBC TV 'Arena' Production, 1985) *18, 30, 45, 74–75, 96, 109–110, 118–119, 121*
Lover Come Back to Me 133
Lover Man 132
Lubin, Arthur *81*
Lucie, Lawrence *39*
Lyons, Jimmy *104*
Lyttleton, Humphrey *121, 122*

MacInnes, Colin *9*
Macolm X *9, 11*
Man I Love, The 45
Mancini, Henry *128*
Mandy Is Two 131
Markham, 'Pig Meat' *45*
Maryland, My Maryland 82
Mayer, Louis B. *81*
McCarthy, Albert *104–105*
McCleary, Tex *118*
McDaniel, Hattie *79–80*
McGloughlin, Virginia *93*
McKay, Claude *22*
McKay, Louis *99, 106, 110, 114*
McKinney, William *17*
McRae, Carmen *84, 113, 115, 127*

Mean to Me 131
Mellers, Wilfrid 119, 134
Mencken, Henry L. 14, 16-17
Mercer, Mabel 76
Mezzrow, Milton 'Mezz' 59, 87
Middleton, Tony 129
Mili, Gjon 95
Miley, Bubber 25
Mills, Florence 22
Millstein, Gilbert 101
Miss Brown to You 36, 132
Mitchell, Red 99
Moanin' Low 131
Monk, Thelonious 102
Monroe, Jimmy 90, 118
Moore, Monette 31, 32
More Than You Know 131
Morgenstern, Dan 108
Morrison, Allan 109
Morton, Benny 65-66, 120, 131
Muggles 85
Mulligan, Gerry 85, 90, 104, 134
Murray, Albert 65
My Man 117-118
My Sweet Lady 9

Nanton, Tricky Sam 25
National Association for the Advancement of Coloured People (NAACP) 10, 32, 55, 79
National Urban League (NUL) 10, 21
Navarro, Fats 88
New Orleans (1947) 81-84
Newton, Francis (Eric Hobsbawm) 57
Newton, Frankie 52
Nice Work If You Can Get It 134
Norris, George W. 25
Norvo, Red 99, 133
Now Baby or Never 133
Now They Call It Swing 131

Obendorfer, Mrs. Marx 59
O'Brien, Father Peter 18
O'Connor, Father Norman J. 111
O'Day, Anita 64, 85, 90, 97, 114-115, 127
Oliver, Joe 'King' 58
One For My Baby 132
Ottley, Roi 25

Parker, Charlie 85, 87, 95
Parnell, Jack 100
Patrick, Dorothy 82, 83
Paul, Les 95

Pepper, Art 85
Peterson, Oscar 95, 127, 132
Piaf, Edith 123
Pinfold, Mike 76
Pinky (1949) 81
Placksin, Sally 63, 64
Pleasants, Henry 123-124
Please Don't Talk About Me When I'm Gone 101, 134
Powell, Adam Clayton, Snr. 60
Powell, Bud 85, 88
Porgy 132, 133
Postif, Francois 107
Preston, Jerry 29
Quill, Gene 135

Raskin, Milt 132
Ray, Johnny 128
Redman, Don 17
Reefer Man 85
Riffin' the Scotch 36, 129
Roach, Max 125
Robeson, Paul 22, 48
Robinson, Bill 'Bojangles' 22
Roosevelt, Franklin Delano 40
Roots 17
Rosenberg, Ethel and Julius 50
Ross, Annie 111
Ross, Diana 10
Rowles, Jimmy 116, 127, 132, 133
Russell, Luis 32
Russell, Pee Wee 102
Rushing, Jimmy 61, 102, 133

Saddest Tale 46, 133
Sanders, Charles L. 107, 113
Schaefer, William Donald 128
Schiffman, Frank 43-44
Schiffman, Jack 34-35, 55, 98
Scott, Hazel 45, 48, 107, 113, 127
Scott, Tony 133
Sendin' The Vipers 85
Selznick, David O. 79
Shapiro, Arthur 133
Shapiro, Nat 19
Shavers, Charlie 132
Shaw, Arnold 75, 91
Shaw, Artie 30, 65, 68-75, 127
Shuffle Along (1921) 22
Simon, George T. 65, 66, 69
Simone, Nina 115, 122

Sims, Sylvia 76, 90, 113, 127
Sinatra, Frank 9, 50
Singleton, Zutty 82
Sissle, Noble 22
Smith, Bessie 18, 22, 25, 32, 35, 47, 58, 86, 123
Smith, Carrie 115
Smith, Charles Edward 53
Smith, Lillian 55-56
Smith, Tab 52
Smith, Willie 132
Smith, Willie 'The Lion' 29-30, 60
Solitude 131
Some Other Spring 39
Sometimes I'm Happy 135
Song of the South (1946) 80
'Sound of Jazz, The' (CBS TV, 1957) 41, 102-103, 134
'Spirituals to Swing' (1937/8) 32
Springsteen, Bruce 32
'Stars Over Broadway' (1936) 47
Stearns, Marshall 24-25
Stegmeyer, Bill 131
Stormy Weather (1943) 81
Strange Fruit 49-50, 52-56, 131, 132
Sugar 131
Sunbonnet Blue 36
Swing! Brother Swing! 66
Symphony in Black (1935) 45-46

'T'Aint Nobody's Business If I Do 109
Taylor, Arthur 45, 115
Taylor, Billy 89
Tea and Trumpets 85
Teagarden, Charlie 36
Teagarden, Jack 36
Them There Eyes 130
There'll Be Some Changes Made 135
These Foolish Things 130
These N'That N'Those 131
They Can't Take That Away From Me 66
Things Are Looking Up 131
This Year's Kisses 40, 130
Thomas, Doll 45
Thomas, Leon 125
Time On My Hands 130
Too Marvellous For Words 134
Toomer, Jean 22
Travlin' Light 132
Truehart, John 36
Trumbo, Dalton 79
Tucker, Bobby 7, 85, 91, 93, 115-116, 120, 127, 132
Tucker, Earl 'Snakehips' 45

Van Vechten, Carl 35
Viper's Drag 85
Vrbsky, Alice 110, 111

Waldron, Mal 103, 105, 110, 116-117, 127, 132, 134
Walker, Alice 11
Walker, T-bone 59-60
Wallace, Michele 118-119
Wallace, Mike 17
Waller, Fats 22, 32, 58, 60
Waller, Fred 45
Warren, Earle 65
Washington, Ford Lee 'Buck' 36
Waters, Ethel 19, 22, 64-65, 81
Watkins, Ralph 90-91
Webb, Chick 22, 43
Webster, Ben 36, 39, 102, 127, 132, 134
Welles, Orson 78
West End Blues 18
What a Little Moolight Can Do 36, 101
When the Saints Go Marching In 82
When Your Lover Has Gone 133
When You're Smiling 130, 131
White, Sonny 52
White, Walter 48
Who Loves You 131
Williams, Bert 22
Williams, Florence 27
Williams, Martin 125
Williams, Mary Lou 63, 64, 107
Wilmer, Valerie 65
Wilson, Dick 29
Wilson, Gerald 119
Wilson, Irene 39
Wilson, John S. 124
Wilson, Teddy 32, 36, 38-39, 43, 54, 127, 131
Winick, Charles 88-89
Witherspoon, Jimmy 128
With Thee I Swing 131
Without Your Love 117, 130
Wood, Berta 104
Worsfold, Sally Ann 135

Yesterdays 69, 131
You Let Me Down 131
Young, Lester 31, 39, 40-42, 84, 85, 95, 102-103, 107-108, 116, 127, 130, 131
You're Drivig Me Crazy 132
Your Mother's Son-in-Law 36, 129
You've Changed 125, 134

Zaidins, Earle Warren 110, 114, 121